BONJOUR! IS THIS ITALY?

A HAPLESS BIKER'S GUIDE TO EUROPE

VELOCE PUBLISHING
THE PUBLISHER OF FINE AUTOMOTIVE BOOKS

Dedication

For Mom, I'm trying

Contents

Prologue

Mike was sitting at the table opposite me looking grim. We'd been discussing the future and had reached the conclusion that it would probably bear an unpleasant resemblance to the present. We were both employed in the nefarious world of financial journalism – a kind of elephant's graveyard where indolent writers came to prostitute their skills to the pimps of the City. The money was good but the work was soul-destroying. Mike was looking especially sorrowful; forced to attend an industry party the night before, he'd consumed more than his fair share of free booze and had accidentally had fun.

"I danced with the editorial director," was all we could get out of him as he stared woefully into his glass and occasionally shuddered. I poured out what was left of the bottle. How much more?, I thought. How much more of this hideousness could the soul endure before the inevitable implosion that would leave me a willing party to this dreadful office hegemony? How long before the routine sets in? Before it seems entirely normal to spend two hours a day pressed up against someone's armpit in a sweltering, packed tube carriage?

An all-too-familiar scene. Left-to-right: Paul, Elliot, Mike, self – another liquid lunch.

My personal nadir had come a couple of weeks earlier, when I'd found myself embroiled in a bitter row over Secret Santa gifts. Just a few short years ago I'd left university full of hope and ambition, and now here I was, furiously defending my right to buy a hip flask for a recovering alcoholic in sales. And what of Mike, my best friend, the closest thing I had to a brother? He, too, was gradually succumbing to the horror, becoming 'one of them.'

Suddenly it all became clear; I knew what I had to do. The time had come to flee.

For a while I'd been toying with the idea of quitting my job and moving to the South of France; of wasting three or four leisurely months idling my life away on a beach, penning an earth-shattering novel and falling in love with a millionairess in her early twenties, whose sole ambition was to marry a penniless journalist and buy him a racing car. It seemed feasible – likely, even. But in such moments one can always rely on the wisdom and jealousy of one's friends to bring one back down to earth.

"You hate beaches," exclaimed Paul, a fellow journalist and long-time friend, who was in the process of adjusting to 'normal' life after spending too many years working in bars frequented by people with names like Harry the Hatchet.

"And people," noted Mike. "Don't forget how much you hate people. You'd have a dreadful time; they'd be everywhere and they'd probably want to talk to you."

"Plus, you'd have to camp," added Paul, with a vindictive smile that quickly faded as the memory of our last camping trip came rushing back. We three friends fell silent as our thoughts returned to that terrible weekend in Monaco, when we pledged never again to sleep under canvas.*

"God, yes," murmured Mike, "never forget Monaco …"

As my friends, Mike and Paul were doing

their level best to ensure I didn't do anything rash or foolish, but I was under no illusion that their motives were anything other than selfish; they instinctively understood what was at stake here: if I was to do this, quit my job and ride off into the sunset, then anybody could do it, and they'd feel even worse about *not* doing it.

There were also practical obstacles that would have to be overcome before any such trip could begin. It was mid-June and, come September, I had planned on moving house, something I felt I ought to be around for. Clearly, if this trip was going to happen, the pieces would have to fall into place fairly quickly.

As luck would have it, a much-needed catalyst lay just around the corner: I was sacked. My editor at the time was a polite and genial fellow who had employed me in the mistaken belief that I knew something about corporate treasury. I didn't. I still don't. During my eighteen month tenure with that publication, just about every piece of copy I filed had to be checked, double checked, and then rewritten. The poor chap's weekends were consumed with weeding out gross factual inaccuracies and phoning contacts to approve quotes which had an uncanny habit of being at least partially contrived.

Amazingly, the best part of twelve months elapsed before I received my first official reprimand. Six months later, when it became clear I was no nearer becoming an expert on treasury, I was put on a two-month trial, after which I was warned that: "serious action would have to be taken."

But it was hopeless: I simply could not find it within myself to care about any of the things I was supposed to care about, so I decided to do the decent thing. Partly to save my own sanity and partly as a gesture of goodwill to my editor, I decided to resign. By a quirky twist of fate, I was fired the next day.

And so I found myself sitting at home

*A dreadful affair (for Mike at least), discussed in detail in chapter 5

in the middle of summer, with a cold beer in my hand and nothing better to do with my life than buy a couple of maps and plan an extended vacation around Europe. I booked my bike – a Suzuki SV650S which I'd bought on Valentine's Day as a present to myself – in for a service, and began looking through various travel guides in a bid to determine a decent route: I never succeeded; Europe is simply too big and diverse for such a structured approach. I could have spent the rest of the year trying to decide which of a thousand destinations would prove the most satisfying, and still missed 99 per cent of what the continent had to offer. Instead, I decided to head for the middle of France, and then choose whether to bear right towards the Pyrenees, left for the Alps, or continue straight on toward the beaches of the Côte d'Azur. Rather than defining a route, I'd let the journey unravel as I went along.

The only caveat to this spirit of recklessness would be the certainty that, at some point along the way, I would have to pay a visit to Stuttgart. I knew nothing about the place other than that one of its residents was an art student whom I'd met earlier that year at a birthday party in Camberwell. Her name was Nina and she looked like Nico of Velvet Underground fame. We'd hit it off and come dangerously close to a relationship before she'd decided to return home to Germany for the summer. I determined to visit her at some point: it would be a nice gesture, a friendly gesture, a gesture that might persuade her to sleep with me.

And so, one sunny August morning, I strapped a tent and some luggage to my motorbike and rode down to Dover,

5.30am, Camberwell, south London. The Suzuki ticks over while, out of shot, I try to cram one more loo roll into my rucksack.

whereupon I boarded a ferry and bankrupted myself with the purchase of a coffee and croissant. Quite a while later, I rode off the ferry and into France – Calais to be precise – which is where this story begins …

The route that eventually unravelled.

1

The road to Rouen

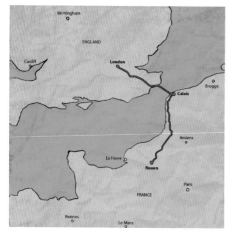

4th August

Actually, the story doesn't really begin in Calais because, frankly, Calais is horrible. The journey began in Calais, but the *story* begins in Rouen, an altogether much more interesting place.

Rouen is a beautiful city located about 150 miles (240km) south of Calais along the A16 motorway. It was pretty much razed during the Second World War, although you wouldn't believe it today. A painstaking restoration process has returned a substantial chunk of the city centre to its pre-occupation grandeur, making it a charming and memorable first stop on my trip.

As the capital of Upper Normandy,

Rouen is perhaps best known as the place where Joan of Arc was burnt at the stake 600 years ago. A big metal cross marks the spot where that unpleasantness occurred, and the city devotes much of its tourist literature to the heroine and her flaming demise.

However, to my mind the city's wonderful architecture – its stunning churches and cathedrals, and the endearing Gros Horloge, an imposing and rather ostentatious medieval clock tower – make for more interesting sightseeing. Built in 1389, this astronomical wonder tells simultaneously the hour, day, and phases of the moon, with each day of the week represented by a Roman God, accompanied by one or two signs of the zodiac.

I suppose it was the medieval equivalent of one of those watches that flash and bleep and do everything but tell the time. I'm sure more than one 15th century merchant stood fuming underneath that clock, certain he was late for an appointment but unable to determine just how late because the hour hand pointed to Mars and the minute hand to Tuesday ...

Rouen is one of those places that, having visited once, you wonder why on earth you haven't been before. However, as I'd never visited previously I was keen to find somewhere to park my bike and take stock of my journey so far.

Like most large towns, Rouen is a

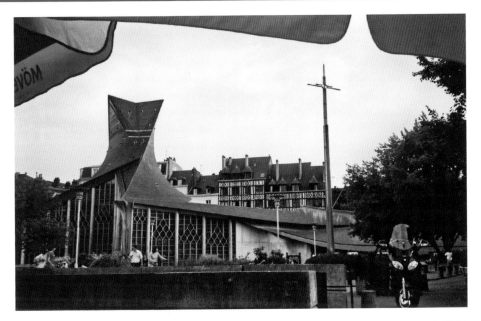

This is where Joan of Arc was burnt at the stake. Not the most attractive memorial, it has to be said.

nightmare to navigate, particularly on a motorbike. It took about two hours of riding around in something like circles before I learnt the most important lesson of the trip: whenever you arrive at a new town or city, always make a beeline for the tourist information centre (they're usually located in the middle of whichever town or city you find yourself in, and are usually pretty well signposted).

The lady at the information centre was very helpful; unnecessarily so, some might say. She kept me talking (or rather, she kept talking to me, I've no idea what she was on about) for the best part of half an hour, and when I finally managed to flee, I did so under the weight of a hundred folding maps,

The impressive, if slightly confusing, Gros Horloge.

Rouen's full of wonderful and historical buildings like this.

Top half of a stunning cathedral ...

... and the bottom half. That's the trouble with magnificent buildings: they're never built with rubbish photographers in mind.

13

A home away from home: my view for the best part of a month.

brochures and pamphlets. Still, she was kind enough to point me in the direction of a cheap and cheerful hotel near the train station which I found with remarkable ease. I booked a *chamber pour une nuit avec salle de bain*, and – with literally nothing else to say – dragged my luggage up three flights of stairs before cracking open a bottle of red wine and collapsing on the bed, a big, idiot grin writ large across my grimy face.

I was actually doing it! Here I was, sprawled out on a cheap hotel bed in a far away city, just me and my motorbike and a bottle of wine, waiting to see what life would throw at me. Part Dennis Hopper, part Peter Fonda, albeit on a Japanese bike with a full face crash helmet. I resisted the urge to call home, keen to revel in my solitude for at least 24 hours and, after a very welcome shower, decided to go for a stroll around this strange foreign world, imbibe its weird customs – and hopefully find a Pizza Hut!

I spent the next couple of hours wandering around the city, taking in the various sights, stopping every now and again for a relaxing drink, but mainly worrying about my bike. The SV650S isn't a particularly desirable machine, but it was all I had and, in the run-up to my trip, I'd heard countless horror stories about bike theft in France, which, if the tales were to be believed, was pretty much a national pastime.

Conveniently, the Suzuki's underseat storage area is just big enough to accommodate a hefty chain and padlock – it's always a good idea to chain your bike to something, even if it's just a tramp – and this, coupled with a front disc lock and an alarm, meant it was pretty much theft-proof. Even so, I couldn't escape the nagging fear that as I sank my third beer, my pride and joy was being wheeled into the back of a van. I decided to return to the hotel earlier than planned to check on her. As a result, I managed to miss quite a bit of what Rouen has to offer, but I can certainly recommend a visit to the wonderful Cathédrale Notre Dame de Rouen, one of the most beautiful buildings I think I've ever been in.

Despite missing some of the most exceptional medieval architecture in France, I was hugely relieved to find my bike shackled to the post where I'd left it. Maybe it was the glow from the setting sun, or maybe it was the half bottle of wine and five beers, but the SV had never looked better than it did there in the cool French evening light: the jet black, slightly bulbous semi-fairing exposed the dull silver engine casing, like a satin dress slipping off an elegant thigh. Well, not really, but in my drunken state I found myself lapsing into that strange, singularly male state of mind that equates fast bikes and cars with the female form. I'm sure Freud would have an explanation for it, but honestly, I don't think I want to

While I didn't spend long enough in Rouen to see half of what it has to offer, I can recommend a visit to the following places. Cathédrale Notre Dame: the subject of a series of paintings by Monet and an awesomely beautiful building. Gros Horloge: one of those things that's worth seeing because: a) it's historically interesting and architecturally impressive; and b) it's bound to crop up in Trivial Pursuit one day. Market Square where Joan of Arc was burnt: not the most interesting of monuments but you wouldn't go to Ireland and not have a Guinness, would you?!

hear it. Anyway, for whatever deep-seated psychological reason, I couldn't resist the urge to throw an ungainly leg over the tank and sit there a while, watching the world go by, just me and the Suzuki.

A while later, having kissed her goodnight and retired to my room, I took out my maps and planned my route for the next day. I decided that, rather than rush on down through France, I'd detour via Le Mans to take a look at the legendary racetrack. According to my map it would be a straightforward and pleasant ride, and I went to bed that night full of booze and bonhomie.

2

Cross-town traffic

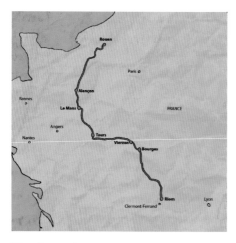

5th August

The relatively short journey from Rouen to Le Mans is straightforward, to say the least. The A28 connects the two cities, and one need never deviate from its path. Needless to say, I got completely and utterly lost, and after a day's riding was still some 25 miles (40km) north of my destination, although I didn't realise this at the time.

As I rode around the little town I believed to be Le Mans, I began to grow quite frustrated at the absence of signposts to the world-famous circuit. More annoying still was the apparent ignorance of the locals: every time I stopped to ask for directions I was met with furrowed brows and blank stares. An entire community was completely blind to this iconic racetrack which sat on its doorstep – or so it seemed.

Finally, having convinced at least ten residents that they really ought to seek out and visit this local treasure. I retreated to a very cheap hotel, whereupon the proprietor politely informed me that I was, in fact, in Alençon, a not unpleasant little town that has nothing in the slightest to do with motorsport. I felt rather foolish. In fact, I would like to take this opportunity to apologise to the many residents of Alençon whom I quietly cursed that day. It appears that it was I who was at fault, after all. By way of an apology, there follows a brief introduction to a town you may never have heard of (or may have lived in for a while without realising).

Alençon is the capital of the Orne region and was, until 400 years ago, the lace capital of Europe. Today, it is best known as the place that used to be the lace capital of Europe 400 years ago, although it also has a very pretty, 15th century tourist information office.

I shouldn't really have been surprised by my ineptitude. Getting lost comes naturally to me; I'm compelled by some unique, rebellious instinct to ignore completely the advice of navigators and road signs. Why, I cannot say, but if a knowledgeable local informs me that the direction I should take involves the first turning on the left, I will

Mom in the Spitfire: happy days.

thank him kindly and then endeavour to drive straight past that road and pick up the third turning on the right. Then, after two hours of furious confusion and torn maps and the quite unnecessary cursing of the kindly person whose directions I ignored, I will find myself in an altogether different part of the world than I expected, and my day will be ruined.

I remember one particular journey to Stockport, just outside Manchester. Mike and I were heading there from Sheffield in a less than reliable Triumph Spitfire. The journey took in a pleasant drive along the infamous Snake Pass, which, as its name suggests, is a rather dangerous, serpentine route full of flowing bends and blind crests,

that connects Sheffield to Manchester. (Interestingly, it seems the road originally took its name from a nearby pub, the Snake Inn, but such is its popularity with serious drivers and bikers that the pub has been re-named the Snake Pass Inn, leading to the curious situation of the road being named after the Inn, which is now named after the road.)

Anyway, it's a stunning route and all the way along it I didn't get lost once. Unfortunately, as we neared Stockport, the road split into multiple lanes and, after a bit of frantic map reading, Mike shouted at me to hold fast in the middle one. Naturally, upon hearing this I drifted steadily to the left and we quickly found ourselves heading in the wrong direction. A rather heated exchange ensued during which, I'm sorry to say, Mike allowed his temper to get the better of him. He cast doubt on the authenticity of my driving credentials, suggested, even, that a monkey would prove a more convincing pilot. He then made some rather disparaging and hurtful remarks about the state of my mental wellbeing. I pointed out that if he had wanted to walk home he need only to have asked, and that I'd only invited him along in the first place to provide a counterbalance to a slightly deflated tyre on the driver's side. The resultant long and sombre silence continued all the way back to Sheffield.

Back in Alençon, I decided I couldn't really bear the prospect of getting lost again, so I had a quick stroll around the town and, upon discovering that there wasn't much to do, grabbed some beers and headed back to the hotel for an early night. Not exactly the 'born to be wild' spirit of adventure I'd hoped for, but when you've spent all day looking for something in the wrong town – a town which you didn't even know you were in – you just have to accept defeat.

6th August

Unsurprisingly, given it was only about 40 kilometres away, it didn't take me too long to reach Le Mans the next day, although trying to find the famous track and museum was a different matter. I'd entered Le Mans from the north, but the circuit is located at the south of the city. Unfortunately, I'd also arrived bang in the middle of morning rush hour.

From the word go I was hopelessly lost, and it quickly became apparent that the city's commuters were not in tolerant mood. Like an ant in the middle of a football pitch I swerved this way and that, attempting to avoid furious motorists while scanning road signs for any hint of direction. Cities aren't pleasant places to ride in at the best of times, due to the sheer number of risks you

encounter, but when you're lost, stressed and tired, mistakes become likely, and mistakes on a motorbike tend to hurt (especially when they involve forgetting you're in France and turning *left* onto a busy roundabout instead of right … it seems that Lady Luck was riding pillion on that occasion).

Having received the sort of wake-up call that could feasibly raise the dead, I decided to call it quits: I rode the Suzuki onto the nearest pavement, took off my crash helmet and sank to the ground next to the bike, exhausted and broken at 9am.

Then an unusual thing happened: an angel appeared out of the traffic in the guise of a rough-looking chap on an old Honda CB500. He stopped next to me and gestured to the madness behind him, "Eez fun, yes?" he said, with a big grin. I replied that if by 'fun' he meant a complete fucking nightmare, then, yes, it most certainly was! We chatted briefly and I explained, in sub-GCSE French and via steering wheel gestures, that I was looking for the Le Mans racetrack, which he kindly offered to lead me to. I couldn't believe my luck. Thanking him profusely, I pulled on my lid and fired up the Suzuki.

Unfortunately, my saviour had neglected to mention that he was suicidal, and that he had chosen this very day – the journey we were on, in fact – to be his last on this earth. He rode like an absolute lunatic and it was only by following suit, ignoring every conceivable sense of self-preservation, that I was able to keep him in sight. We squeezed through gaps in the traffic that wouldn't have been possible had I had a slightly bigger breakfast that morning, and gambled with our – and every other road users' – lives at each and every junction. It quickly became apparent that my guide viewed traffic lights as a form of street decoration, pleasant enough to look at but of no practical value to a man in a hurry. In our wake a thousand car horns beeped

Finally, having risked life and limb to get there, the impressive entrance to the Le Mans circuit.

furiously, while just feet ahead pedestrians dived this way and that, thrilled no doubt to have had their dull morning's routine injected with such excitement. Through all of this my insane companion rode with heroic abandon, and I remember noting in a fleeting moment of calm that I hadn't seen his brake light come on once since he'd launched me into this hell just ten minutes earlier.

Finally, we pulled up outside the gates of the famous circuit and I all but staggered off my bike; I was literally shaking as I walked over to where my guide had stopped, unsure whether to thank him or hit him. I didn't get the chance to do either, however, as he flipped up his visor and, pointing behind him – and without a trace of irony – shouted

"French drivers, zey are facking crazy," before dumping his clutch and shooting off down the road with a quick wave, accompanied by a not insubstantial wheelie and the sound of blaring car horns.

The museum that sits next to the racetrack at Le Mans is something of an Aladdin's Cave for a motor racing enthusiast. Although perhaps not quite on a par with the museum at Donington Park, the display at Le Mans more than adequately represents the vast range of machines that have been put through their paces on the famous Circuit de la Sarthe, since the first 24 hour race was staged back in May 1923 (and won by André Lagache and René Léonard in their 3 litre Chenard & Walcker).

The achingly beautiful Porsche 917 Longtail failed to finish the 1971 24 Hours race, but when something looks this good you can forgive it almost anything.

It's a bit *Wacky Races* but the unique, hub-steering Elf X was ahead of its time.

Like its American counterpart, the Indianapolis 500, Le Mans has witnessed both triumph and tragedy. 1955's race included the most horrific accident in the sport's history when eighty people died after Pierre Levegh's Mercedes struck the rear of an Austin-Healey driven by Lance Macklin. After slamming into a grass verge, the Mercedes shed its engine, which then slewed into the packed grandstand, carving a devastating path through the hapless spectators.

Motorsport can be cruel, but it can also be uplifting and inspiring, and the 1969 Le Mans race is a perfect example of this. Back then, the race always began with the 'Le Mans start,' whereby the drivers lined up opposite their vehicles and, as the lights turned green, sprinted across the track, scrambling into their cars and firing up the engines in a bid to be first away. As exciting as this spectacle undeniably was, the powers that be finally banned it in 1970 after it was discovered that many drivers, in an effort to secure a tiny advantage, were not bothering to do up their safety harnesses until they reached the long, 200mph+ Mulsanne Straight, whereupon they would fasten their harnesses whilst holding the steering wheel between their knees.

In protest at this dangerous practice, the famous Belgian driver Jacky Ickx decided to amble, rather than sprint, to his car at the start of the '69 race, pointedly fastening his safely harness before firing up the engine – he went on to win the race.

Before leaving Le Mans, I wanted to take a quick ride along the above-mentioned

Parked up on the Mulsanne. The temptation to cane it and spend the next month in jail was almost irresistible.

Mulsanne Straight, which is a public road when the racetrack is not in use. The route from the museum to the Straight is as follows (it may appear that I have simplified it: I assure you I have not): turn right out of the museum, take the second road on the right, ignore any mischievous instinct suggesting you are heading in the wrong direction and, after a kilometre or so, arrive at your destination. Not so difficult, really, but, in trying to find that stupid stretch of road I gained a pretty good insight into what completing the 24 hours race must feel like.

The Mulsanne itself is a strange affair. For a petrol-head aware that he's on one of the most famous pieces of racetrack in the world, the everyday traffic is more than just a nuisance; it feels almost sacrilegious to be travelling so slowly along this hallowed stretch of Tarmac. The only upside to riding along at what feels like walking pace is that you're able to take in the details: all those little signs and roadside images that you've seen on TV so many times. If you let your mind drift a little – probably best to pull over first – you can just about imagine what it must feel like tearing down this narrow strip of road, pushing 250mph in a Porsche 956, the trees nothing but a green blur in the corner of the eye, the little houses and churches flicking past in an instant. Flat out. Pure concentration. Darkness falls and the clouds roll in; rain begins to stream off the windscreen, visibility down to a few precious

Some very impressive topiary in, I think, Tours (apologies if elsewhere).

Judging by the garage in the background, that's an old R6 sporting the famous 'Shrubbery' livery.

metres but speed undiminished, plunging into the blackness … it takes a special kind of madness …

Heading south from Le Mans the temperature began to rise and the greenery of northern Europe is replaced by wilting vegetation and harsh scrubland. I made my way toward Tours, then across to Vierzon and Bourges, passing through countless small, dusty, sun-bleached villages before the heat got the better of me and I decided to rest for the night in a pretty little town called Riom.

I suspect Riom is very old and probably the scene of many interesting historical events. Sadly, I can elaborate no further because, having dumped my bags in the first hotel I could find and taken a quick shower, I spent the entire evening making notes in a nearby pizzeria and getting happily drunk on cheap red wine.

3

Here comes the sun

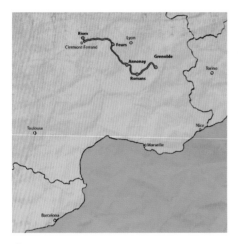

7th August

Grenoble is a beautiful city set against a magnificent Alpine backdrop, and the route from Riom is great fun to ride: it twists and turns and undulates with growing severity as the Alps loom ever-larger in the distance. It's a terrific journey, especially if you can avoid the motorways and instead take the sweeping, cross-country route down through Feurs, Annonay and Romans, flat out at times and always ready for a freak mountainside gust to catch you broadside and heave you into the path of an oncoming truck. But the roads are so smooth and virtually empty that big speed is almost a pre-requisite, at least on the larger roads where the throaty V-twin will wind up

to 120mph without a glitch and sit there comfortably while you tuck down on top of your tank bag, a big grin spread across your face.

Pin the throttle on a downhill stretch and the needle edges slowly toward 130mph, but now the SV's engine is straining. The red line approaches for both bike and rider, as instinct begins to tighten the muscles until your arms cease to function as useful shock absorbers. At this point you have to step back, at least mentally; not necessarily by rolling off the throttle, but by consciously relaxing, forcing the brain to release its stranglehold on the sinews, to unlock the talons clenched around the handlebar grips and let the forearms cushion and iron out the natural imperfections of the road. Then everything becomes slower, easier and, paradoxically, faster.

It was late afternoon when I finally arrived in Grenoble but no one had told the sun, which was clearly enjoying itself and in no rush to curb its mid-day ferocity. In fact, with the cooling wind whistling through my visor all day long, I hadn't realised just how hot it was until I pulled up outside the tourist information centre and instantly started to cook in my leathers. It was absolutely scorching, which made the next hour and a half even more gruelling as I rode around the city trying to find either a hotel that wasn't full or a campsite. Being

It doesn't get any better than this.

Grenoble, a very pretty city and the perfect base for a biking holiday.

August in the South of France, the former option was essentially wishful thinking, so I made my way slowly across town towards Seyssins, a little suburb to the south west of the city, where I eventually (don't bother looking for signposts) found Camping des Trois Pucelles.

Honestly, I don't think I'll ever be able to find words to express the sheer relief of getting out of those leathers. I draped them over the SV, which had coped admirably with the sweltering conditions, and set to work putting up my tent. Then, just a few hours later, I went and had a shower, grabbed some beers from the bar, and spent what was left of the evening outside my tent, relaxing under the stars.

8th August

It turns out there's a knack to manipulating a motorbike jacket into a usable pillow, and I finally mastered it at about four o'clock in the morning, having spent the preceding five hours mainly awake and uncomfortable. I awoke the final time at about 8am and unzipped my tent to find most of the campsite already up and about and enjoying the morning sunshine. There wasn't a cloud in the sky and, as I stumbled out of my tent and turned to face the day, I was met with

An inimitably French scene.

the most spectacular view of the Alps, which, in my groggy state, I'd completely forgotten were there. It was one of those moments that define a trip like this: clear blue sky, blazing sun and snow-capped mountains, all within thirty seconds of waking up. It was quite inspiring.

I decided to head into Grenoble for breakfast and then explore the city on foot before riding up into those stunning mountains. Remembering the sweltering heat of the previous day, and with only a short ride into Grenoble ahead of me, I decided to ditch my leathers and adopt the continental T-shirt and jeans approach to riding, which allows for a great suntan providing you don't fall off and require a skin graft. Having turned my tent upside down (literally) searching for sun block and discovering I had just enough as to be completely useless, I fired the SV into life and made my way into the centre of Grenoble, full of excitement and anticipation of what the day ahead would hold.

My first port of call was a supermarket to purchase some sun block, but I'd forgotten it was a Sunday and consequently most of the stores I came across were closed. I eventually found a general store which looked hopeful – it had beach-wear and buckets and spades outside – but as it turned out, no sun cream. I couldn't believe it. Every other useless product you could imagine sat on those shelves, from comedy glasses to snorkelling accessories; they must have revelled in the eclectic nature of their stock. One can envisage the proud owner ushering in a bus-load of tourists, shaking each by the hand and proclaiming in a booming, triumphant voice:

"Come hither one and all, for this store will fulfil your wildest dreams. What's that you require, sir? A basket of figs and some engine oil? Third aisle on the right, my good man. Pardon, madam? A silk kimono bearing the embroidered likeness of Buzz Aldrin? Why, I have one here. Unicorns? Step this way sir." After a while, one of the tourists, a mild-mannered sort of chap with a reddish forehead, would venture politely: "Excuse me, monsieur, your shop is truly remarkable, exceptional even in the scale and diversity of its stock, but could I enquire as to the whereabouts of the sun block?" The owner would ponder this request for a while and then call to his sons in the warehouse to "bring forth the Crème De Soleil." After much confusion and stumbling and swearing, a sheepish teenager would emerge and, head bowed, whisper into his father's ear:

"Papa, we 'ave no sun block," at which the proprietor would fall silent and stare into the distance for a long time, as his eyes filled with tears. And then, an agonising wail would trickle from his anguished mouth and, falling to his knees, he would implore forgiveness from the startled crowd. Finally, if he had an ounce of decency within him, he'd run out the back and kill himself for his dreadful oversight.

Certainly, this is what I wished upon a number of Grenoble merchants that day as I dashed from shadow to shadow like a deviant for the best part of an hour trying to avoid the sun. Eventually, I did find a small chemist that stocked sun block and, judging by his prices, the proprietor understood the gravity of my situation.

Despite few shops being open, I had a very enjoyable day wandering the quiet streets, taking in the beautiful architecture and stopping every now and again to gaze up at those stunning mountains. Eventually, I came across the Bastille Cable Car ride, which, for a few euros, will take you right up into the hillside via a pod-like cabin that sways precariously as you travel up and over the city's roofs and river.

The view from the top of the Bastille hill

is quite breathtaking as the beautiful city stretches out in a vast expanse, dissected by a massive arterial highway. The hill itself was, according to my guidebook, first fortified in the Middle Ages and is covered with the most extensive 19th century military fortifications in France. It's a fascinating place, with numerous caves to explore and various hideaways that have served as armouries and whatnot over the last few hundred years. And encircling this spectacle, the brooding, foreboding Alps, where once Napoleon and his army trekked, resplendent in their epauletted trench coats, marching with grim determination over those treacherous passes.

What a sight that must have been, the brilliant general and his tacticians proudly riding ahead, flanked by drummers and pipers, and behind, stretching away into the distance, a great mass of devoted troops poised on the brink of military history.

Perhaps it was this snapshot in time that the man in front of me was considering as he lent, rather purposefully, against the balcony of the mountainside restaurant in which I was seated. He was a ponderous chap, and, with one foot perched precariously on the barrier, he gazed out upon the city below, adopting a rather contrived pose which implied that he alone could appreciate the gravitas of that magnificent view. This annoyed me, and I was about to pack away my book and leave when an amusing thing happened. A little boy of perhaps seven years of age, who had obviously had enough of

Tremendous views from the Bastille hill.

Absolutely terrifying, the pods swing about perilously and you can't help but think there used to be more of them!

this chap's silly posturing, ran up behind him and tried to murder him. The little fellow ran smack into the man's back and, owing to the latter's ridiculous pose, unbalanced him, causing him to very nearly topple over the barrier to a certain death. The man wasn't happy about it and, having finally regained his equilibrium, immediately flew into a rage, promptly dropping his camera over the edge, which made him madder still. The poor little boy was soundly berated until his mother appeared. She was a big lady, and it appeared for a moment that the Grim Reaper would claim the fellow after all. She went ballistic, pinning the poor man up against the railings, demanding that he apologise to both her and the child before sending him on his way, suitably chastened.

It was excellent entertainment and I only wish I'd been able to sneak a photo.

I remained on the hillside balcony for some time; it was very hot and very beautiful, and every time I tried to leave I couldn't resist one final glance at that spectacular view. Eventually, I managed to tear myself away and hopped into one of the bizarre pod-cars that swayed disconcertingly in the mild breeze as it made its leisurely descent.

Back at the campsite, however, my day was about to take a turn for the worse.

In hindsight, I put it down to sunstroke, which I must have contracted up on the mountain and become delirious, otherwise I'd never even have contemplated using the dreadful swimming pool. Things began to go wrong before I'd even entered the pool enclosure. I managed the disinfectant footbath okay, but then could not for the life of me work out how to open the gate. Eventually, a small child of no more than six was kind enough to explain the mechanism to me and I nodded my thanks, hoping none of the other bathers had witnessed my confusion. I placed my book and towel on a handy sun lounger and then leapt into the pool wearing my shorts. Let me repeat: I leapt into the pool wearing my shorts, that is all. Yet, judging by the horrified looks on the

Grenoble's a fantastic place, full of character and perfectly located. It's a city with a keen interest in outdoor pursuits, whether that be cycling, skiing or enjoying a nature reserve. I really enjoyed my brief visit and have been back a few times since. For bikers it makes a great base for a holiday, especially with the Route Napoleon so close by. For more details, visit: http://www.grenoble-tourism.com/

faces of my fellow bathers you'd have thought I'd just sold their children into slavery and donated the proceeds to the Kitten Culling Society. My crime? To have had the audacity to wear shorts, not designated swimming trunks, in the pool. "Sir!" an almost hysterical-sounding voice shouted from the crowd, "eet is not permitted to wear shorts in the swimming pool!" He said it again, his voice fraught with agitation. "You must wear swimming trunks to enter ze pool!" It was a horribly embarrassing incident that left me with little option but to gather up my belongings and retreat posthaste to my tent. Grabbing my book and towel, I squelched my way from that watery hell, nodding my thanks to the little girl who opened the gate to let me out.

4

Meat is murder

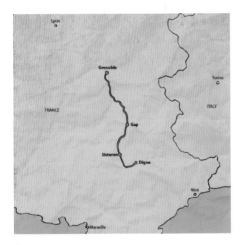

9th August

Having drowned my sorrows of the night before and awoken with a pounding headache, I breakfasted on paracetamol and coffee, and decided to push on down to the coast. I'd enjoyed Grenoble but I was keen to get to the seaside and have a splash about in the Med for a few days, so I packed up and consulted my map.

Surprisingly, there's no direct route from Grenoble to the coast, which must be a pain if you live there but is an absolute delight if you're a biker with time on your hands, as it leaves you no choice but to ride some of the best roads in Europe. Among these, the Route Napoleon – officially known as the N85 – is a biker's dream. A couple of

The start of a very special journey.

Corps – one of countless pretty little towns dotted along the Route Napoleon.

friends had mentioned it to me before I'd left London, and the enthusiasm with which they spoke about its many twists and turns was contagious. I'd made a mental note to try and find it if I happened to end up nearby and so, armed with some rather convoluted directions from the campsite owners, I headed off in search of this legendary road.

It took me about two hours to make my way across Grenoble and finally pick up signposts for the N85, although, frankly I've no idea how I got there. What I can say is it was worth the effort.

The Route Napoleon takes its name from the path the famous French leader took when returning from exile in 1815. It stretches about 300 kilometres, from Golfe Juan on the coast to Grenoble, via Grasse, Seranon, Digne, Sisteron, and Gap (and a wealth of other small towns and villages); as far as I can tell, it doesn't run straight for more than 100 metres at any point. It's an

extraordinary piece of highway, for which the term 'twisties' – as in "Did you take the motorway?" "Nah, I've just dropped a tooth on the front sprocket so I took it through the twisties and nearly killed myself" – could have been invented. It's full of every kind of bend, from beautiful sweeping third gear scrapers to unsighted switchbacks that seductively beckon you in like sirens and then tighten savagely, forcing you wide of your apex (and into the path of oncoming traffic). Thankfully, the route is also extremely quiet, meaning you can get away with a little enthusiastic riding, though if you do come a cropper, you probably won't be found for hours, if not days.

It's not just the road that makes the N85 such an essential ride: the scenery – a mixture of lush forest, sheer cliffs, and shimmering rivers at the bottom of immense, ragged canyons – is something to behold. Each twist and turn reveals yet another extraordinary

My overriding memory of the Route Napoleon – mile after mile of glorious bends (note murderous little pothole that almost had me off).

Welcome to the pleasuredome.

Dramatic scenery, perfect weather, stunning roads. And we get the M40 …

vista; it's so beautiful that you have to force yourself to concentrate on the road, not the view. It would be so easy to let a lingering glance become your last, especially as you get closer to the coast, where the canyons become ever more intimidating. There are few guardrails to speak off, and in many places all that separates you from the bottom of a ravine is a quaint rustic wall, which is just high enough to save your bike as you fly over the handlebars and plummet to your death.

But as I'm sure many readers will agree,

this is what makes such places so special: the knowledge that your fate lies entirely in your own hands, not in the office of some local bureaucrat or officious health and safety officer.

That said, rounding a blind bend to find a pile of rocks in your path and a 300ft drop to the right does tend to focus the mind somewhat, and it wasn't long before that reckless spirit, which had my knee-skimming Tarmac outside of Grenoble, was replaced by an altogether more respectful riding style.

At this more sedate pace it quickly became clear that I wouldn't be parking up at the seaside come evening, especially as I found myself stopping every ten minutes or so to take photos. Instead, I decided to enjoy the route over a couple of days, stopping off midway at an interesting little town called Digne les Bains (interesting, that is, in terms of its geology, which may or may not be an oxymoron).

10th August

Owing to its unique position at the transition point between the Alps and the plains of Provence, a significant chunk of Digne les Bains is protected because of its geological importance (it's full of fossils). Its location has endowed it with numerous hot springs – to which the town owes its name – which are supposed to be good for respiratory problems and rheumatism, containing, as they do, sulphur, calcic (lime and calcium), and strong minerals. They are also, according to a surprisingly innocuous note in my guidebook, lightly radioactive.

Despite its small scale, Digne is full of character: a maze of alleyways and steps, and higgledy-piggledy houses painted in long-since faded pastel hues. The church of St Jerome stands above the town square, and looks old and beautiful in the way that churches ought to. Like a miniature Grenoble, Digne nestles amidst harsh, mountainous scenery, which is threatening, beautiful and awe-inspiring in equal measure.

A number of campsites are dotted around Digne that, in itself, is a pleasant little town in which to spend an evening; it's not, however, somewhere you'd necessarily choose to spend a couple of days – but of course I didn't know that at the time.

As the sun slowly sank behind those majestic mountains I wandered around the town, stopping now and then for a beer and generally unwinding after the day's ride, which had been as exhausting as it was exhilarating. Riding a motorbike isn't a passive activity, it requires constant input, not only from your hands on the throttle, clutch and brake, but from your entire body, as you shift your weight this way and that to combat the centrifugal forces that want to keep the bike going in a straight line. If you're pushing on and keeping up a decent pace you'll be adjusting your position non-stop, your feet pushing down on the pegs, shifting your mass this way and that to help the bike turn in. Twist the right wrist and tuck down behind the screen, holding on tight as the revs rise and the wind starts tugging at your helmet, then hard on the brakes, arms tense, supporting your body weight while the nose of the bike dips and you slide yourself sideways, knee stretched out to meet the road as your slider scrapes along the Tarmac. Then back on it again, elbows in, pulling yourself forward, keeping the weight over the front wheel to stop it rising under acceleration. It's a fantastic feeling; come rain or shine, as the saying goes: 'It's all about the bike.'

The next morning over breakfast I toyed with the idea of pushing on to the coast. But as I was in no rush, and because I didn't yet know there was nothing to do in Digne, I resolved instead to head into town and see what entertainment I could find.

Three hours later, on my way back to the campsite, having done precisely bugger all, I rode past a sign directing me to a Geopark. I wasn't quite sure what a 'Geopark' was but it sounded more interesting than sitting in a tent warding off grasshoppers, so I pulled into the car park, anticipating a fun-packed afternoon of discovery.

Now, some months later, sitting here at my desk writing this book, I am still struggling to think of a time when I have been more disappointed. Those signs on the side of the road should have read 'dull fossil bin' or 'old rock shop,' as that's pretty much all that the various rooms housed. It was only upon my return to England that I discovered the geological importance of Digne; lacking this knowledge at the time, I couldn't help but wonder what in God's name the point of the place was. Furthermore, the Geopark sits at the top of quite a steep hill, and I was more than a little vexed to discover I'd staggered up there under the baking midday sun just to look at some stupid trilobite. To be fair, if geology and natural history are your thing then it's probably quite an interesting place, and the views from outside the tourist shop at the top of the hill are very impressive. But if you're hoping for robotic monkeys (and I was), you're wasting your time. Honestly, I must have ignored a billion years of natural history in the half hour or so it took me to locate the exit, and to this day I don't feel like I missed a single interesting thing.

Actually, that's not strictly true. One room housed a number of fish tanks full of weird and wonderful life forms, including a sea cucumber and an animal that looked for all the world like a big gob of spit. With nothing better to do I sat and pondered those bizarre creatures for a while, watching them bob about aimlessly in their little tanks. I fell to questioning the strange machinations of nature, the seemingly endless variety of beast and foul that walks or crawls or finds some other way to shift itself around this world. And I found myself asking … why? Why bother being a sea-cucumber? What kind of a life is that? Floating around with nothing to do all day but avoid bumping into your best mate who looks like he's just been heaved up from the chest cavity of a man with terminal bronchitis?

I did try and feign interest in a couple of bones and a miniature Jurassic swamp, but in the end had to admit defeat. I bought a plastic diplodocus and made my way back to the campsite.

On my way I happened across a chip shop (I'm sure the French have a grander term for it, 'restaurant de la frites' or something, but I'm sticking with chip shop). Anyway, with nothing but bread and crisps back at the tent, I stopped in for a late lunch. I'm a vegetarian, a concept still mocked openly in many parts of the world – not least by my friend, Bob – although in Britain vegetarianism is pretty much established nowadays and finding a meat-free option on a menu isn't that difficult. To the rest of Europe, however, and France in particular, the concept is anathema. A French waiter will stagger backwards and sink to his knees when you tell him of this bizarre fetish.

"None at all?" he gasps, incredulous.

"No, none at all," you patiently explain.

"No pork?"

"No meat whatsoever, I'm afraid," you reply with slight irritation.

"Chicken?"

"No, nothing with a face or parents," you continue through gritted teeth.

A long silence ensues, during which the poor fellow wracks his brains for some option that has not recently ceased to breathe. Then, eureka! He offers up the fish menu.

So you can probably guess what happened in the chip shop. I asked for some pomme frites, nothing else, just chips, but was not surprised when I left the shop and opened the bag to be confronted by a huge steak sandwich. I plucked out as many uncontaminated fries as possible and gave the steak to a stray dog, which showed none of the gratitude I'd expected …

While the Geopark at Digne wasn't my cup of tea, the scenery surrounding it is especially attractive.

5

Mike fought the tent (and the tent won)

11th August

After a day-and-a-half in Digne, which I shall never get back, I rose early and, with the sun blazing above, made my way back onto the glorious Route Napoleon with a view to reaching Nice by late afternoon. Believe it or not, after Digne, the Route gets even better, with astonishing views across the rugged terrain and mile after mile of beautiful, empty road. I rode for about an hour before chancing across a French Resistance museum, situated pretty much in the middle of nowhere, but with a jet fighter parked outside to grab your attention.

I can't imagine that museum gets much custom – all the visitor guides were faded and dog-eared and the ageing receptionist seemed vaguely surprised to be confronted with someone who was not just asking for directions. It's a shame because it's a pretty interesting place. The main entrance is guarded by what appears to be a decrepit old French lorry but which, on closer inspection, turns out to have a huge great machine gun mounted on the back of it. Inside, much had been made of old letters, maps and uniforms of the heroes of the Resistance, along with some Nazi memorabilia, including pictures of the young German soldiers – boys, really – killed by French bullets but murdered by Hitler.

I spent a good half hour examining the various artefacts and found it quite a moving experience. I'm afraid I don't know much about the activities of the Resistance, certainly not in the South of France, and while I can't say I came away fully enlightened, the museum certainly helps preserve the memory of those brave men and women who sacrificed so much for a future they would never know.

On my way out, I stopped to admire the jet that was so incongruously placed in the dusty car park (and which I've since learnt is a Fouga Magister, a very successful French training aircraft built in the late 1950s). As I poked around the undercarriage I felt a tap on my shoulder; it was the old boy from the reception desk. He nodded hello and then gestured up at the cockpit. He didn't need

How this little place stays up is anyone's guess, but I can't think of anywhere I'd rather live.

Better than any arcade machine, although the SV has more luggage space.

Hard to imagine now but this heroic little car actually fought the Nazis.

to elaborate; I scrambled up the ladder like a rat up a drainpipe and all but toppled into the pilot's seat, unable to believe my luck.

The cockpit was full of every dial, knob and lever you could hope to find, and I began flipping switches and thrusting the joystick about like a madman. Moments later I received another surprise when the old fellow reappeared holding an authentic helmet for me to wear; I thanked him profusely and pulled it on, unaware of what a tit I now looked. I stayed in that seat for 20 minutes or more, my mind flitting between various fantasies which ranged from flipping

You can't imagine how cool I thought I looked at this moment.

the bird to the pilot of a MiG 21 whilst engaged in a 4G negative dive to locking my X-foils in attack position and barrelling into the Death Star's trench, evading laser fire and TIE Fighters, and questioning the wisdom of disregarding my targeting computer.

I could have stayed there all day and probably well into the night but for my new best friend who, realising I wasn't going to leave of my own accord, started banging on the canopy in a manner that suggested he wanted to go home. I flicked a few more switches, made a quick, unauthorised flyby of the control tower and then, having guided home a panic-stricken Ghostrider, made a near-perfect landing on the pitching deck of the USS Enterprise, before finally, in every sense of the word, coming back down to earth.

It was a real treat and I only wished I'd been able to adequately thank the old chap for allowing me such an experience. Unfortunately, I could only repeat *merci* while vigorously shaking his hand and grinning like an idiot. Then I donned my own (more fetching) crash helmet and fired up the Suzuki. As I rode away I turned and shouted "You can be my wingman anytime," but I don't think he heard me.

A few hours later, as I neared the coast, the isolated beauty of the Route Napoleon gradually faded; traffic increased and the barren rocks gave way to wealthy-looking homes with swimming pools and big gates. Battling through traffic on the wrong side of the road in 40 degree heat is no fun, so I was very relieved when I finally found myself in the middle of Nice, with the sea just a short walk away. Sadly, my dream of finding a secluded beach quickly evaporated. The city was heavily congested: in fact, it reminded me far too much of the hustle and bustle of London and everything I was trying to

The definition of tranquillity.

escape. Rather than endure the busy August crowds, I decided to head along the coast to a town called Menton, about 15 kilometres east of Monaco.

Menton had been our home when Mike, Paul, Duncan, Thom and I had driven from London to Monaco and back in three days to watch the Grand Prix. Afterwards we worked out that not one of us had had more than eight hours' sleep during the entire trip, although Thom did manage an extra few minutes' shut-eye on the way home (whilst driving). To this day, Mike has not forgiven him for that little indiscretion, but his annoyance at Thom's somnambular escapade pales in the face of

his outright fury at what we still refer to as 'the tent incident.'

A little background is necessary here. Prior to our journey to Monaco, the five of us had convened at my house in London, where, over a few beers, we discussed practicalities, including sleeping arrangements. Paul and I were to share Mike's tent, while Thom would sleep in the car and Dunc would stay in his brand new, two-man tent. After a while, however, Mike began to express concern that his old tent may not actually be roomy enough to comfortably accommodate three people (a fact that he now vigorously denies); consequently, Dunc and I decided that I would stay in his tent. Admittedly,

Mike was not consulted on this issue, but at the time it seemed a minor logistical point not worth mentioning. That is how I remember it happening; Mike's recollection differs.

When we finally arrived at the campsite in Menton at about 11pm after a 20-hour drive, it's fair to say the atmosphere in the car had become a little tense. Keen to put some distance between us we dispersed to different ends of the campsite. 20 minutes later, having put up our tent, Dunc and I retired to the bar, where we were joined by Thom a while later. After an hour or so of pleasant drinking we decided to call it a night, at which point we realised that neither Mike nor Paul had yet joined us. Deciding they must have gone to bed, we headed up to their pitch to wake them and say goodnight.

But they weren't asleep; in fact, they were some way from that restful state. I should say Mike in particular had never been more awake in his life. There he stood in the moonlight, struggling under the canvas, surrounded by tent poles and pegs and trying his best to ignore the encouraging cheers emanating from the sizeable crowd that had gathered to witness the spectacle.

Judging by Paul's body language, which exuded a queer mix of depression and fear, they'd been at it for a while. Mike, on the other hand, was anger personified. I calculated that, by the time we arrived, he'd been fighting that tent for over an hour and it showed no sign of yielding.

It was a monumental battle: indeed, Thom was so inspired that he ran back to the bar and grabbed three chairs, which we placed a respectable distance away and sat on to enjoy the show. When Mike finally spotted us watching from the wings, he expressed himself very crudely. Frankly, I was embarrassed by his language and Dunc commented he was glad the crowd was foreign, so probably couldn't understand the

more esoteric terms being voiced. In fact, we were so shocked by Mike's vulgarity that we had to return to our tents and go to bed.

The next day, when we came to wake Mike and Paul and saw the true scale of the previous night's carnage, we each felt a little uneasy (Thom said he felt an unusual sensation and likened it to that which he'd heard others describe as 'guilt'). The tent – actually, it was more of a bundle – was encircled by beer bottles, food wrappers and cigarette butts, and the extent of the litter suggested that the crowd had grown considerably after we'd left. From what I could make out – Mike wasn't speaking much – they'd finally got a single pole to stay put in its vertical position at around 2am, at which point, exhausted, hungry and humiliated, they had simply thrown the canvas over it and crawled underneath to a mighty cheer from the revellers, some of whom had apparently remained long into the night in the hope that the solitary pole would collapse.

So I couldn't help but smile when I realised the campsite I'd been directed to by the friendly tourist information staff was the very same one where my two close friends had suffered such humiliation a few years earlier. As a sort of tribute, I chose almost the exact spot that the battle had taken place to erect my own tent. As it turns out, the earth in that particular patch is extremely rocky and, baked by the August heat, was as hard as concrete: it wasn't complete incompetence that had so plagued Mike and Paul, after all.

Thankfully, I'd brought along a little hammer for just such an occasion, which I made a mental note to mention to Mike when I got home; I knew he'd be happy for me.

But pride, as they say, comes before a fall, and it turns out it wasn't just the rocky soil that had hampered my friends: that patch of ground is cursed and whoever happens upon

The exact moment when a thousand angry ants marched into my tent.

it is destined to a horrible fate. In my case, I put my tent up on an ant hill.

Unaware of the suffering that was about to befall me I headed into Menton for some dinner, but unsurprisingly, given the time of year, was heaving with tourists. Instead, I grabbed a cheese sandwich, a bottle of wine and some crisps, and spent the evening on the rather pebbly beach, listening to the ocean and pondering the stars above (it was quite strong wine).

6

Not waving but drowning

I woke early the next morning to find myself an itching red lump of misery. I'd been bitten all over, including numerous attacks to my face, which looked hideous. I was only grateful Mike wasn't around. I packed up quickly, keen to avoid human contact and, visor firmly closed, rode from that evil place toward Monaco, where I hoped I could find a chemist.

It's an easy ride to Monaco along the winding coastal road, and you can't help but imagine what it would be like were this your daily commute (as opposed to the pothole-ridden, diesel-soaked hell that is the London road network). The views are stunning: to the right, tree-covered cliffs, speckled with luxurious houses and apartments, and the

The full Monte Carlo: free to those who can afford it, very expensive to those who can't.

45

More of these in Trafalgar Square!

sparkling blue ocean to the left. And then Monte Carlo, snuggled into the coastline and glistening in the sun; it's impossible not to be impressed, at least from a distance The roads are sinuous and busy, but it's all so affluent and glamorous you don't really mind. It's just nice to be a part of it.

If you follow the coastal road (which starts off as the D52 from Menton but then evolves through a raft of different numerical names which would be very confusing were Monaco not so well signposted) it'll take about three quarters of an hour, but there's a much quicker train service that runs all along the coast and is probably a better option if you're planning on staying in one place for a few days.

As it was, I arrived in Monaco at about 10am with a view to having a quick ride around the streets before heading on further round the coast toward Italy. Like many of its wealthy and glamorous neighbours along the Cote d'Azur, Monaco isn't a particularly interesting place if you can't afford to patronise the casinos or sunbathe on a yacht. Personally, without the distraction of the Grand Prix, it's not somewhere I'd want to stay more than a few hours, so I set about locating Boulevard Albert 1er, which is where the Formula One cars take position at the start of a Grand Prix (the grid markings are in place all year round so you'll know when you get there. It's a great feeling when you suddenly realise you're riding over the exact same spot where Senna sat in his McLaren, waiting for the lights to turn green).

But for the absence of an 'M' this would have been a great photo.

Like the Mulsanne Straight, there's a peculiar feeling that comes with riding along what you know to be a racetrack, but which the locals regard as just another road (most of the time, anyway). I chugged along at a snail's pace up toward St Devote, surprised by the steepness of the gradient, and then along past the casino and round the awkward Mirabeau right-hander, before plunging down toward the famous Loews hairpin (about the only place you'll be doing the same speed as the Formula One boys); then right again to enter the claustrophobic, narrow, low-ceilinged tunnel. Unfortunately, on the exit of the tunnel, just before the Tabac section, I came across roadworks which diverted me around and away from the twisty swimming pool complex, before bringing me back onto the track just before the tight right-hander of La Rascasse, the last corner of the lap.

It was on the exit of La Rascasse that I heard what sounded like a poorly maintained machine gun behind me; I turned to see a gorgeous Ducati 916 indicating to pass so I eased off and waved him by, mainly to get a better look at the bike. We exchanged nods, as bikers do, and he sped off. And I followed. We were certainly not racing, but, as I pulled in behind the flashing blue lights of the police car, I wondered if the prisons in Monaco were in keeping, style-wise, with the rest of the city. I figured I might be in for a treat: a couple of nights rent-free in a five-star cell with proper toilets and showers; maybe even with breakfast thrown in. I'm sure it's an EU requirement these days.

Unfortunately, the gendarme was in no mood for jokes, and as he began examining my bike and making disparaging noises, I prepared myself for the worst. Inspection over, he commanded me to remove my helmet, which turned out to be a stroke of luck because the poor fellow almost fell over himself in shock when I did. My face was a mess of nasty red blotches and I was sweating profusely; I looked as though I had the plague. At that point I believe any thought of being in close proximity to me – either filling out endless forms or cooped up in the back of his car – fled from his mind, and instead, his focus changed to getting me as far away from him and his people as quickly as possible. He thrust a piece of paper in my direction – to this day I have no idea what it says – and beat a hasty retreat to the safety of his car. Once there, he wound the window down a crack and either reprimanded me or gave medical advice, I'm not sure which, before ushering me on my way with a quick, unambiguous hand gesture.

An hour or so later I reached San Remo, having ridden back through Menton on the D52 from where I picked up the busy A10 autoroute, which I was glad to get off after about 18 miles (30km).

As usual it was baking hot and I was itching like mad in my leathers, so I began searching for a hotel where I could relax, take a nice cool shower, and forget all about camping for a night.

I decided to stay in the first hotel I could find, which happened to be the Hotel Plaza. I parked up, grabbed my luggage and climbed the five flights of stairs that took me to the reception desk, where I was informed by a disinterested idiot that the hotel was full. I suggested in simple English – which I hope he understood – that the hotel might like to consider putting a sign saying as much at the bottom of the stairs. Frustratingly, the next four hotels I found (none of which had a reception on the ground floor) were equally full, so I resigned myself to the inevitable and set off across town to locate a campsite. If you ever find yourself in a similar situation in San Remo, may I suggest you don't waste your time searching for the campsite, and ride on to the next town where, if you're

lucky, they'll have heard of signposts. I went back and forth along the small but busy road that runs through San Remo for about an hour before I finally found the campsite, which was only a couple of kilometres out of town but the entry to which was concealed by what had to have been intentional camouflage. I wasn't in the best of moods when I finally found the reception desk and even less happy some ten minutes later.

"Zat will be 33 euros, sir," said the lady on reception.

I stared at her blankly and then, after some quick mental arithmetic, explained that I was only staying for one night and just wanted to camp, not establish a permanent residence.

"Yes, sir, 33 euros a night: zat is ze price."

"I don't want a chalet or anything, just a pitch." I replied incredulously.

"Yes, sir: to camp is 33 euros for one night."

I was gob-smacked. Thirty three euros! For one night! I was livid; unfortunately, I was also now so desperate to get out of my leathers and put some cream on my bites that I had little choice but to hand over the cash.

The thief took my money and then beckoned over one of her accomplices who led me to the car park where I locked my bike and unstrapped my luggage. I was about to ask him how far the campsite was when I noticed a number of tents erected rather precariously in the spaces reserved for the cars.

"What are those for?" I enquired.

"Zey are tents," he replied, his tone a mixture of helpfulness and staggering condescension.

"I know that," I said, "I have one here. I've just paid one of your colleagues a week's wages to live in it for the next 12 hours. What I want to know is why those tents are here in the car park."

Not the actual campsite: believe it or not, this is significantly better.

Every fibre in my body was begging him not to say what I knew he was about to.

"Zis is both ze car park and ze campsite, sir."

"A campsite, yes, but surely not *the* campsite," I persisted. "Not the site that is costing me 33 euros a night?"

A slightly heated debate ensued, after which I was left in no doubt that – as a consequence of it being August, when all of France took its holidays, and thus everywhere was extremely busy – the car park was indeed doubling up as a campsite. And not only a campsite, but the most expensive and uncomfortable campsite I had ever set eyes on. To make matters worse, the car park was no more than 15 yards from the rocky seafront, which left it exposed to ocean gusts that threatened to sweep me to my death during the night. The only consolation was that any ant colony would have packed up long ago and moved somewhere more comfortable.

Friday 13th August (!)

I awoke early to the sound of a surprisingly rough sea crashing against the rocks just yards away. People were already up and about and enjoying the rather boisterous waves, so I decided to have a quick breakfast and join them. As I emerged from my tent, a friendly-looking chap nodded hello, then paused and looked me up and down.

"They are perfectly suitable for swimming in," I muttered impatiently, recalling the incident in the swimming pool a few days earlier.

49

"Pardon?" he replied, with a startled expression.

"Oh, I'm sorry, I thought you were going to comment on my shorts" I said, rather embarrassed now.

"Not at all," he responded, his air suggesting it was not for him to dictate what others should wear, no matter how ridiculous they might appear. In fact, his concern was that I was going to go swimming at all.

"You know, it *is* rather rough out there this morning."

"Yes, but those folk are swimming," I countered, pointing to what in hindsight I can only assume were mermaids, "So I guess it's safe to do so?"

"Oh yes," he answered, with a look that implied it was anything but. "I'm sure it's fine; just be careful, that's all." And with that he nodded goodbye and went on his way.

I put my towel down and considered his warning: it did look rough; terrifying even, but I could definitely see children bobbing about out there and they didn't appear to be drowning. As I sat and watched, more and more people entered the water, laughing and splashing about in a manner which made me feel a tad foolish. Eventually, I decided to hedge my bets. I grabbed my belongings and began edging my way along the rocky shoreline with a view to finding a suitable place to sit and let the waves wash up around me. (I have since discovered that this seemingly harmless strategy is a very effective way to get yourself drowned and, in light of the following events, I consider myself massively fortunate not to have ended up that way.)

To begin with the waves played fair, crashing upon the larger boulders out to sea but dissipating by the time they reached me to gently wash up around my waist. Even so, I could feel their force rocking me back and forth slightly each time the water rose around me. Still, it was a pleasant enough sensation and I closed my eyes to bask in the warm sun.

I considered my journey so far, the distance I'd travelled and the sights I'd seen. I dwelt upon the beautiful scenery and the fantastic roads, and began to ponder whether I shouldn't extend my trip a little, to take advantage of this wonderful opportunity. Life, after all, is short, and these moments of sunshine and happiness can be few and far between. And then, of course, there was Stuttgart and Nina; a beautiful, intelligent girl who clearly liked me. Maybe she'd ask me to move in with her! I knew for a fact her parents had a Mercedes. Perhaps her father would warm to me and offer me a job in his factory testing sports cars. Yes, that would almost certainly happen, I was sure. I smiled at nothing in particular and lay back on the rocks, feeling content and optimistic, ready for anything life could throw at me.

The next moment, all such thoughts were literally flushed away as I found myself submerged under a raging, foaming torrent of brine that wrenched me from my rock and dragged me, flailing, out to sea. By sheer luck I managed to grab hold of something solid that anchored me long enough for the waves to momentarily subside, allowing me to catch my breath. Then it happened again: the sea surged over me, smashing me against the rocks before sucking me backward, out into the ocean. I clutched at the rocks with all my might as the sea roared above, and for a few seconds, I really thought I was going to die. I remember being astonished by the sheer power of those waves and the accompanying swell; I was completely helpless, utterly at the sea's mercy, and far beyond any kind of fear I'd ever experienced before. Unable to move, or even breathe, all I could do was hold on and hope that my grip would outlast the surging tide. With that terrible roaring noise filling my ears and my eyes shut tight, my fingers started to slip across stone and I knew, absolutely, that there would be no way back if I lost my grip.

In those few short moments I felt what I can only describe as a profound, gut-wrenching fear that I hope I never experience again. Miraculously, at that moment, the torrent abated enough to allow me to heave myself back up onto the rocks and away from the sea's murderous reach.

Only when I was sure those terrible waves could no longer grab me did I collapse on the warm, dry stones, able at last to catch my breath and wiping away tears of relief. When I finally opened my eyes I discovered I was bleeding quite substantially from a bevy of cuts and grazes that extended pretty much over my entire body. Still, I considered myself lucky that I wasn't halfway to Corsica already.

Behind me, a middle aged lady who must have witnessed the entire spectacle was kind enough to point out my misfortune to her neighbours. She called down to me, commenting on my bruised and bleeding form.

"Was that from the rocks?" she enquired politely and rather unnecessarily. Had I the strength I might have hurled her into the sea. As it was I replied meekly, and with considerable understatement:

"Yes, it's rather choppy out there."

Back in my tent I nursed my wounds and, being in rather introspective mood, composed this depressing little tale, inspired by the houses high up in the hills of Monte Carlo:

Once upon a time there stood a large, empty mansion on top of a hillside. The mansion had been quiet for many years, since its last inhabitants had all died of a rare strain of poverty. The house sat cold and quiet and sad, wishing it could enjoy once again the sound of children playing and cups and saucers clattering in its kitchen. But most of all, the house wished it could hear the sea crashing on the rocks below. It was too high up and too far away to hear the wonderful sounds of the mighty ocean as it lashed the rocks in winter and tickled them in the summer. Oh how the house wished to hear the sea.

Then, one day, a family came to look at the house, to inspect its walls and survey its foundations. The house was so happy as the children ran excitedly from one room to the next, and their parents talked about how they'd renovate the lounge and bring the old place back to life with a dab of paint here and there. From the big upstairs windows ran two trickles of water; the surveyor said this was dodgy guttering but, in actual fact, it was the house weeping tears of joy. And in the background, just faintly, the house was sure it could finally hear the sea.

As the years passed by and the children grew up the house was happier than it had ever been. Now, when the children were fast asleep, it could definitely make out the symphony of the waves below and it seemed to the house that the ocean's gentle tune was growing louder with each passing year.

Then, one day, a serious-looking man in a black suit arrived and he and the family convened in the lounge. The usually happy family looked miserable. The house couldn't quite make out what was going on, such was the racket coming from the sea, but it knew something was very wrong. A couple of days later, a large van pulled up outside, into which the family moved all of their furniture. Gone was the beautiful old clock from the hall, and the ornate lampshades from the lounge; even the Persian rug from the kitchen disappeared and the house suddenly felt empty and sad. The family wept and hugged one another and said goodbye to the old house they loved so much. With a final sorrowful wave and a whimper from the dog as she clambered into the back of the car, they were gone.

Once again the house stood empty and

alone, but now the sea roared below and its bellowing only scared the house. Cold and fearful, the poor old house looked out across the waves and longed for better days when the sea was just a faint whisper. But the cold and vicious ocean had no pity, and every day it edged closer, until one day, those cruel and powerful waves began to hammer against the cliffs below and the miserable house felt as though it were being eaten alive. Finally, the rocks upon which it stood began to crumble, and the poor old house tumbled into the sea and was no more.

I must admit, penning this fine tale did little to cheer me up, so I hobbled over to the bar and watched *The Empire Strikes Back* in Italian.

7

Don't worry, be happy

14th August

For the last couple of days I'd been debating whether or not to push on down to Rome or head east across northern Italy to Ravenna, and then up to Venice. From what I'd heard, Venice is very pretty, but smells and is sinking, whilst Rome is full of pickpockets, but offers more for the casual tourist. It was a tough choice. In the end I decided to base my decision on the weather and, as it appeared to be raining in Venice and baking in Rome, I began plotting a course south.

Rome's about 400 miles (650km) from San Remo if you take the most direct path, which involves a not inconsiderable ride along the A1 autoroute from Firenze. Instead, I decided to take my time and hug the coast, stopping in whichever town I happened to be near come evening.

After a long day's ride, partially along the busy A10 to Genoa, then on the more peaceful coastal roads towards La Spezia, I finally arrived at a very pretty little seaside town called Lerici. It had been an enjoyable, if uneventful day; just me and the Suzuki, happily riding along and enjoying the sunshine and great roads.

In Lerici, I chanced across a campsite called Camping Maralunga, which overlooks the ocean and is about as peaceful as you could hope for in Italy in August. Despite being almost full, the manager was able to find me a tiny space which I gratefully accepted. Unfortunately, my pitch completely overlooked that of a young German couple who were clearly hoping to

Y776 HMV – sold by mistake. If you know of its whereabouts, please get in touch.

enjoy some solitude. I ignored them as best I could, but inevitably, every time I did glance in their direction they would be kissing or she would be getting undressed or hanging out her underwear. In the end I began to feel like a degenerate and decided the only way I was going to convince them otherwise was to embark on a polite introduction and apologise for my inadvertent voyeurism. As it turned out, they were both very friendly and we retired to the bar for a quick drink, after which I decided to finish off the evening with a stroll into town.

It was dark by the time I left the campsite and I thought it wise to ask directions from the site manager before leaving. He advised me of a short cut that would reduce my journey into town to a mere 15 minutes; however, it deviated significantly from my map and appeared a little convoluted.

"It looks a little convoluted," I said, "are you sure I won't get lost?"

"Oh no," he laughed. "There is only one turn, I assure you it is impossible to get lost."

And you know what? He was right. I spent the evening wandering around the little shops and bars, enjoying the harbour views and feasting on a huge pizza that demanded a vat of wine accompany it. Then, after ensuring the bar I'd been frequenting enjoyed a giddy day's profit, I made my way back up to the campsite and to bed.

15th August

I'd enjoyed my night in Lerici so much that I decided to spend the next day there, too, and was very pleased that I did. It's a reasonably busy little town with a lovely harbour, overlooked by an imposing castle which I felt compelled to explore.

A small, angular building of Genoese construction, Lerici castle houses both Saint Anastasia's chapel and a quite remarkable collection of plastic dinosaurs,

The castle overlooking Lerici harbour.

Terror from the deep: not the most inspiring exhibition I've ever been to.

certainly on a par with the Geopark in Digne. These unconvincing beasts formed the main attraction of the Museum of Geopalaeontology; a brilliant name for a woeful display of dinosaurs created to illustrate the type of creatures that once stalked the area. Judging by the calibre of the display, Lerici must once have been home to some of pre-history's most laboured and uninspiring beasts; a place where evolution couldn't really be bothered. A land filled with dinosaurs that kept falling over and bumping into each other. I doubt a single creature that inhabited that area ever had a documentary made about it.

Still, the castle itself is well worth a visit, with terrific views out over the bay. (May I also recommend the public toilets at the top of the tower, which are clean and spacious, and make for a refreshing change if you've been camping for the last couple of weeks.)

Sitting in the castle's restaurant (you thought I was going to say toilet, didn't you?) I watched the tourists and locals mingle, and it struck me how calm and relaxed everybody seemed. There was none of the frantic pushing and shoving that you get in London's busy tourist sites. I pondered this for a while and concluded that it could probably be explained by the near perfect climate. A few moments additional thought resulted in the following hypothesis which, to my mind at least, is absolutely and fundamentally credible.

Britain, in particular southern England, receives a mixed bag of weather, which means we are never really prepared for either sun or rain. Should we be lucky enough to enjoy a long, hot summer, people complain about the heat and get sunstroke, and the councils impose hosepipe bans and everyone gets irritated and annoyed. If, on the other hand, July and August are cloudy and wet, we curse the skies above our heads and bemoan our sodden lot in life. We doubt we will ever see the sun again and complain about the heating bills. So no one is ever really content and, consequently, southerners adopt a rather cynical approach to life.

In stark contrast, the Mediterranean people are far less bitter about life in general. They know that, whatever happens, the sun will keep shining and the sea will never ice over, so why worry? Why push and shove your way around a castle when a pleasant and relaxing stroll will afford the same result? It's an attractive alternative to sweat and irritation, although this approach to life does have one significant drawback: a near American absence of irony. If, for example, a child were to fall over in the street and begin to cry, the Italian would completely fail to see the humour of it. The Englishman, by contrast, would be doubled up in hysterics, his cup of bitterness replenished for the day. On the other hand, were a clown to tumble on a banana skin, the French audience would rupture with mirth, while the English spectator would look on, bemused and slightly irritated.

My theory perfected, I finished my coffee and headed off around the port in search of fresh challenges.

Aside from its splendid castle and picture-postcard views, Lerici has another claim to fame: it's the place where the poet Shelley moored his sailing ship, the *Don Juan*, whilst residing in the small town of San Terenzo, a couple of kilometres up the coast.

Shelley and fellow poet Byron could often be found sailing their vessels around the gulf of Spezia, and generally living it up in decadent manner until Shelley met his end amid a raging storm that took the *Don Juan*, the poet and his crew to the bottom of the ocean. Shelley's body was washed up ten

Feeling quite pleased with myself having just perfected one of the great hypotheses of our time.

days later on the beach at Viareggio, a few kilometres down the coast.

Actually, the mention of Byron reminds me of an altogether unpleasant incident which took place at the Hotel Byron, located on the seafront near Lerici's harbor. To cut a long story short, I found myself needing the loo just as the whole of Italy was shutting for lunch. Whatever I'd eaten the night before had decided that it wished once again to experience the beauty of the outside world. Somewhat panicked, I hurried from one 'closed' sign to the next before happening upon the unfortunate Hotel Byron. I say unfortunate because what happened next was indeed mad, bad and dangerous to know, and to make matters worse, I couldn't locate the flush. I searched high and low but it was nowhere to be seen. I pushed on random bits of wall and waved my hand over the cistern hoping to find some discreet sensor, but nothing worked. Eventually, I conceded defeat and, with an altogether hypocritical nod of goodwill towards the lady on reception, I hurried out the door and never went back.

8

Lean on me, I won't fall over

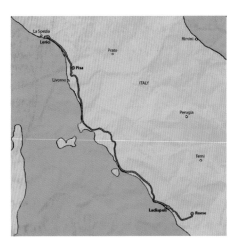

16th August

Ladispoli lies about 30 miles (50km) outside Rome – and some considerable distance from the Hotel Byron – and thus seemed as good a place as any to set up for the night after another day's ride along the beautiful Italian coastline.

I had fully intended on being in Rome by late afternoon, but had underestimated how long it would take me to ride down from Lerici. Additionally, the roads had been busy and I'd spent longer than intended at the Leaning Tower of Pisa, which lies just off the A12, the main road I'd been travelling along. I hadn't realised that the famous tower is only a small part of a much larger complex of stunning white buildings which form the

The Leaning Tower of Pisa, a breathtaking piece of architecture.

The Campo dei Miracoli – largely obscured by a rather mucky biker.

Piazza del Duomo (or Cathedral Square), a walled area at the heart of the city. The square is also known as the Campo dei Miracoli (Field of Miracles), and it's not difficult to see why. The architecture is stunning; you could easily spend an afternoon staring in wide-eyed disbelief at the beauty of it all. It comprises four main buildings: the cathedral, a baptistery, a cemetery and the famous leaning tower itself, which is actually a free-standing bell tower for the cathedral. Even if it weren't for its precarious angle, the leaning tower would still be breathtaking: it's so painstakingly detailed and delicate, an extraordinary triumph of art and architecture.

Sadly, being on my own, I wasn't able to take a picture of myself holding it up, but I did buy a couple of tacky models (including one that wasn't leaning at all and I hope is a leftover from *Superman III*).

I left Pisa somewhat reluctantly at about 3pm, having spent much longer there than I'd intended, and still hoping to make Rome by evening. I managed to get a little lost on the way, however, and found myself in Ladispoli just as it was getting dark.

I'm afraid I know nothing at all about Ladispoli, except that the campsite I stayed at had a karaoke stage and they weren't afraid to use it ...

17th August

I can't say I enjoyed my brief stay in Ladispoli: the karaoke dragged on quite late and I lay in my sleeping bag quietly cursing the place until I finally drifted off to sleep. The next thing I knew it was half past seven in the morning, the sun was shining, and it seemed like the perfect time to make the short journey along route SS1 toward Rome, the outskirts of which I reached at about 9am.

Rome – or rather its populace – has a

reputation for the sort of extreme driving usually reserved for stunt shows. I didn't fancy battling my way through the rush hour traffic again, so decided to stop for a while and get some breakfast. I bought a slice of water melon from a vendor on the side of the road, grabbed a takeaway espresso, and found a bench on which to enjoy a refreshing, if rather messy, breakfast.

As I sat there, munching away and covering myself in melon juice, the thought struck me that, without really trying, I'd reached a midway point in my journey. This was as far south as I planned to go and my thoughts returned to that early morning run to Dover just two weeks earlier – it seemed so long ago now. Yet, here I was, parked on the outskirts of Rome, eating a watermelon in the sweltering sun. I thought of my friends back home and wondered what they were up to; the usual routine, I guessed. Paul would be chasing stories under the cloud of a horrible hangover; Mike would be facing the weekly press deadline, his reporters cowering under their desks. And my housemates, Barry, Hannah and Laura, all going about their daily lives, no doubt having forgotten that I ever existed. Well, maybe not, but it's surprising how long a fortnight can seem when you're on your own and each day you wake up in a different place. Life seems to move along quickly, and yesterday seems like last year's holiday: a distant memory as you push on toward tomorrow.

And push on I did, though where I was going I had no idea. I hadn't planned on visiting Rome until a couple of days earlier, so had done no preparation whatsoever. I rode around for a while, hoping to spot a tourist information office, but essentially just travelling in horribly convoluted circles. I envisaged spending the next few days in the equivalent of Hendon, never actually discovering the city proper. (Mike and I had done exactly that during a week's holiday in Rhodes. We arrived on the Monday, spent four days thinking Rhodes wasn't all that special, then, by pure chance, found ourselves right in the heart of the splendid old town about five hours before we were due to fly home.)

Thankfully, by sheer luck, I eventually found myself riding alongside the Vatican walls, which enabled me to get my bearings and work out where I might want to base myself. I found a little hotel that didn't seem too expensive, given the time of year, and set about cleansing myself of watermelon.

I had planned on spending two full days in Rome, which, according to my guidebook, was about three weeks less than I needed if I wanted to see everything. But I didn't really want to see everything, just the main touristy bits, so I decided to split the city in half and spend my first day focusing on the Colosseum and some of the bigger churches, while the second day would be occupied with the papal delights of the Vatican and the Sistine Chapel.

Like the Pyramids or Che Guevara, the Colosseum is one of those images that has been scorched onto the public retina by hype and over use, yet the reality is still breathtaking, at least initially. The famous rotunda, with its giant columns and crumbling arches rising up amid the little shops and bars, is so incongruous it could almost be a mirage. For something so aged (it was begun in AD 72) to exist slap bang amid the hustle and bustle of modern day Rome is just bizarre. In truth, I was expecting to find it resting in quiet splendour on some silent hilltop or surrounded by manicured gardens. But the cars rush by, disrespectfully honking their horns, seemingly oblivious to the great chunk of history in their midst.

It's strange how quickly we become accustomed – and then indifferent – to the unique forms that make up our world. Just before I left London, I'd got chatting to a

Reflected in the window of a café, the once mighty Colosseum now seems almost lost amid the hustle and bustle of Rome.

friend of a friend about the prospect of life on other planets. He waxed lyrical about the strange and unimaginable forms that such extra-terrestrial life would take, and how important it was that we plough vast sums of money into space exploration. I said maybe we should concentrate our resources on protecting and conserving our own planet, with its polluted oceans and shrinking forests. But his focus lay beyond Earth: he had tired of the almost infinite variety of life on this planet and craved new excitement. No matter that creatures exist on this planet so utterly different from us that, were they to be presented as such by an intelligent-looking chap with a beard, they could quite easily pass for extra-terrestrials. I imaged my new friend's reaction had he been presented with that glob of spit I'd seen floating about in Digne and been told it'd just plummeted out of the sky in a silver capsule. He'd no

doubt be agog at its unearthly appearance, mesmerised by the environment that could have created such a being. But upon discovering its Earthly origins, he'd instantly tire of it and return to his telescope to stare endlessly into oblivion.

I must admit, I found the Colosseum a somewhat macabre affair: effectively a gargantuan stage for cruelty and murder. Standing there, amongst the other tourists, trying to imagine the horrific last moments of some Christian martyr or brutalised, maimed lion, I felt nothing but shame and sadness. What a horrible way to die.

Moral qualms aside, I was also somewhat dissatisfied with the scale of the building. Yes, it's big – colossal, even – but let's not forget that these people owned half the known world at the time. No doubt in its day, the Colosseum towered over the city, resplendent and mighty; but now, at least after the initial impact has died away, it seems almost lost. I'm sure our descendants will say the same when seated in their mile-high office blocks, gazing down on the tiny London Shard.

I was similarly underwhelmed by the Roman Forum, which I mistook for a building site. The guidebook informed me that it was once 'the most celebrated place in ancient Rome.' I have no reason to doubt this; I'm sure that thousands of years ago it was a grand and ostentatious site where learned men and women came to worship at temples and enjoy exotic feasts. Unfortunately, the few sun-bleached pillars which today jut out of the ground amongst the rubble failed to convey the magnificence of this spectacle, so I went and had a beer instead.

Some time later I said my goodbyes to the Colosseum and its decrepit neighbours and began a long trek across town, unsure of where I was heading but certain of finding something interesting when I got there.

The side streets of Rome were quiet and I felt quite alone as I made my way up a rather steep hill, at the top of which sat a small church. The courtyard seemed deserted and I had the distinct impression it had been that way for many years. According to a little sign, I was in the grounds of the Basilica SS Quattro Coronati, which forms part of a convent and is adjoined to the Chapel of St Sylvester and a 12th century cloister (I didn't know it at the time, but tourists can enter the cloister by ringing a special bell which prompts an Augustinian nun to open a small wooden hatch and pass through a key. A process which, in my imagination at least, resembles the chiming of a bizarre cuckoo clock).

It was at once eerie, sombre and peaceful and I felt duty-bound to step inside and take a look around. And thank goodness I did. While quite small and intimate, the

Mr SPQR – clearly an important fellow back in the day.

Basilica is a beautiful building, far more exotic than I'd expected, but in no way garish or ostentatious (unlike many of the other churches and cathedrals in Rome, more of which later). A beautiful domed roof sits atop the cold stone walls, decorated with

The fourth century Basilica SS Quattro Coronati: an extraordinarily peaceful church with a fascinating history.

layers of cherubs and angels, and culminating in an incandescent sun which, I assume, represents Christ. With the exception of myself and a nun, who sat in quiet reverie below the altar, the building was empty and incredibly peaceful.

I sat for a while and wished I was a religious person. I wanted to chat with the nun, to ask her about God and faith and belief and everything, but I knew it would ultimately be a futile discussion. One either does or does not believe. There is no true agnosticism; that is merely cowardice disguised as contemplation.

Leaving the nun to her solitude, I ambled off down the hill and wandered aimlessly for half an hour or so until I found myself confronted by the imposing façade of the Cathedral of Rome. Known properly as the Basilica di San Giovanni in Laterano (or 'the Mother of All Churches' according to my guidebook) the cathedral is massive and ostentatious on a truly biblical scale. I don't think there is a single inch of wall, ceiling or floor that is not coated in silver or gold; it is a place where the term 'subtlety' has no meaning and it left me with mixed feelings. I was gob-smacked by the splendour of it all, but a nagging sense of worthiness left me questioning how anyone could squander such wealth on such indulgence? It made me think of Orwell and his hatred of the Sagrada Familia in Barcelona: he said it was one of the greatest failures of the Spanish Revolution that the anarchists hadn't burnt it to the ground when they had the chance.

Inside the Basilica the sense of history is almost palpable.

Couldn't work out whether it was his act, or if this human statue was just having an afternoon nap.

You can see what he's getting at – it's the very antithesis of dull and worthy socialism – but really, as a monument, it is almost without equal.

The same can be said of the Mother of All Churches: it is horrific and spectacular in equal measure. Thousands must have starved to death or lived in abject poverty while the church hurled fortunes at such projects, yet for all the inhumanity, you can't help but marvel at its scale and magnitude.

That evening I took a walk around some of the back streets near my hotel and found the shops and stalls packed with an astonishing array of religious tat – holographic postcards of Mother Teresa, multi-coloured plastic cherubs, a miniature globe with the Pope's face depicted as a kind of hideous Pangea spanning the Earth. It was garish and plastic and tacky and would serve as the perfect aperitif for a trip around Vatican City.

9

Going to the chapel

4 0 degrees in the shade sounds like a Bon Jovi album, but was, in fact, the actual, ridiculous temperature Rome was experiencing at the time of my visit. So, having climbed the 320 steps that lead to the top of the dome of St Peter's Basilica, you can imagine how pleased I was to discover from two far less sweaty tourists that there's a lift that will take you most of the way. Still, the view from the top is astonishing and well worth the effort: Rome fills the horizon, stretching out as far as the eye can see, while directly below, the pristine walls of the Vatican encircle the famous Obelisk, once said to have housed the remains of Julius Caesar himself.

Looking down on the spires and domes of this vast city, framed by a brilliant blue sky, you can imagine how God must feel when he gets up each morning. Like most cities, a change of perspective is often all it takes to forget about the hideous practicalities of daily life and fall in love again with the history and culture that defines them. The cityscape on that clear summer's morning was magnificent, and it was fascinating to spot and identify the many churches and landmarks I'd passed the previous day (although the Colosseum, of all things, was not visible from the roof of St Peter's, which perhaps goes to show how that once mighty building has been consumed as the city, and indeed the world, has grown around it).

Far below in St Peter's Square (which is about as inaccurate a geometrical description as there can be) I could just about make out the brightly coloured tunic of a Swiss Guard, the military force which has protected and defended the Vatican since the fifteenth century. Like the Beefeaters who stand around the Tower of London looking a bit weird, the Swiss Guards' menacing presence is somewhat diluted on account of their outlandish, floral garb. One can only imagine the response of these hard-nosed mercenaries when Michelangelo, no less, revealed the uniforms they'd be wearing for the next 500 years or so, which can best be described as Laura Ashley meets Punch and Judy. I refrained from mentioning this, however, as they are still pretty tough customers: during the Second World War, this small group prepared itself to stave off a Nazi invasion of the Vatican that would have seen the Swiss Guards hopelessly outnumbered, and no doubt systematically slaughtered. The invasion never materialised, but that shouldn't detract from the bravery this small band showed in the face of truly appaling odds.

Inside the Basilica, guards dressed in more familiar attire and armed with guns ensured no-one got too familiar with the Pope's treasures. Like the Basilica di San

A God's-eye view of Rome.

Giovanni which I'd visited the day before, St Peter's Basilica appears to be a monument to papal wealth and ostentation first, with God coming a poor second. Inside, it's all brash gold and cherubs, with the notable exception of the beautiful La Pietà – a vision of Mary cradling the dead Christ, sculpted by Michelangelo in the late fifteenth century. It is so utterly perfect that one can hardly conceive of it ever being a clumsy lump of rock. Michelangelo was so proud of this work that he engraved his name on the sash crossing the Virgin's chest; it was the only piece he ever signed. Yet even Michelangelo wasn't averse to employing a little artistic license: apparently, the figures are significantly out of proportion, to the extent that if the figure of Jesus were to scale,

the Virgin, standing, would be sixteen feet tall!

On 21 May, 1972, a chap called Laszlo Toth took a sledgehammer to the Pietà and, whilst proclaiming himself to be Christ incarnate, managed to smash off the Virgin's arm, remodel her nose and chip one of her eyelids. Surprisingly, Toth received substantial credit for his actions from certain artistic quarters, where he was hailed as an iconoclastic cultural terrorist. The Laszlo Toth School of Art was formed in his honour, and Toth became known as 'the Artist of the Hammer,' which is a bit like calling the destruction of Dresden 'town planning with a bomb.' Thankfully, art restorationist Deoclecio Redig de Campos was able to return the sculpture to its

At some point in history, someone must have slid down the bannister leading to the Sistine Chapel.

original beauty, while Toth spent two years in a mental asylum before being shipped home to Australia (proof that there is still a modicum of justice in the world). Today, only a layer of bulletproof glass reminds the visitor of this ugly moment, and Toth's sole legacy is to have made it virtually impossible to photograph the Pietà without the flash ruining the image.

Despite my personal moral qualms regarding the decor of St Peter's, I came away from that place once again amazed at the capability of mankind when we put our minds to something; an opinion soon to be reinforced by the delicate beauty of the Sistine Chapel, the next stop in what was becoming something of a whirlwind tour.

The famous Chapel lies at the end of

a vast and ultimately withering tour of the Vatican Museums, where you can gaze at myriad artefacts and then instantly forget them. It's a shame in many ways that the casual visitor has to spend the best part of an hour traipsing through corridor after corridor of triptychs, urns and paintings, because the experience ultimately detracts from the splendour of the Chapel itself.

Once inside, the Chapel is smaller and darker than you might expect, and it takes a while for your eyes to grow accustomed to the dim light, but once they do the vision is quite spectacular. Unlike St Peter's, or any other church in Rome, the Sistine Chapel doesn't flaunt its wealth: it is modest and alluring, more Audrey Hepburn than Betty Page. Michelangelo's ceiling is suitably

The imposing Castle St Angelo, brooding over the Tiber for the best part of two millennia.

impressive, and it's difficult to determine whether some of the cherubs (or are they angels?) are paintings or relief carvings. The same can be said for the painted curtains which cascade down the walls and which I actually had to touch to make certain they weren't real.

But the crowning achievement of that place, to my mind at least, covers the far wall of the Chapel and captures the imagination in a truly biblical sense: Michelangelo's Last Judgement is an awe-inspiring, apocalyptic masterpiece that manifests every superstitious fear of hell and damnation we learn from infancy. It is the Book of Revelation incarnate, terrifying and huge and captivating in a way that no gilded altar or gold-encrusted vault could ever be. I could

have spent the rest of the day revelling in its detail but, sadly, that's not an option. You're allowed only five minutes or so to bask in the Chapel's glory, before being ushered on your way by the intimidating guards (who, to be fair, do a terrific job of keeping excited Americans quiet).

Before leaving Rome there was one other sight I wanted to see: the Castle St Angelo, an imposing, rotund construction next to the Tiber, originally built as a mausoleum for the emperor Hadrian between 130 and 139AD. Entering the castle via a spiralling rock staircase, a mercifully brief walk brings you out in the main body of the building, where lots of interesting historical artefacts are gathered.

Sadly, that's all my notes said about the

Castles? Tick. Chapels? Tick. Cathedrals? Tick. Catapults? Tick. The author's interest in antiquity begins to wane. Time to move on.

Castle St Angelo, and I fear I may have been tiring of spectacular, ancient sites by this time. However, don't take that as an indictment of the castle per se; it is a splendid structure, from the top of which you get a fantastic view of the Vatican, in itself an excellent reason to make time for a visit.

I decided to crown my short time in Rome with a decent meal in a proper restaurant. Having eaten almost nothing but pizza for the best part of two weeks I decided a change was in order. Then, having examined the menu for all of 30 seconds, I decided it wasn't after all and ordered a massive margarita and a bottle of wine, over which I spent a relaxing couple of hours soaking up the unique atmosphere of this incredible city. Then I ambled* over to the Vatican for a final goodbye and reminisced on what an enjoyable, if exhausting time I'd had over the last two days. My guidebook had listed thirteen essential things to see and do in Rome and I'd visited nine of them. Three weeks indeed!

---

* At least, I remember it being an amble; it may have more closely resembled a stagger.

A room with a view: looking out across St Peter's from the Castle St Angelo.

10

Help!

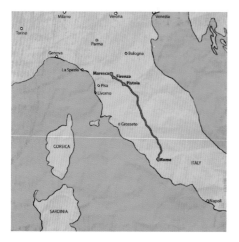

19th August

I felt a little sad to be leaving Rome, in particular, wondering if I'd ever see the Colosseum again. I needn't have worried; in trying to leave that city I must have passed the wretched thing a hundred times, always from a different direction and with an ever-increasing desire to never see it again. Eventually, having exhausted every conceivable incorrect route, I drifted onto the A1 motorway that would take me north for the first time in two weeks.

The plan now was to head along the A1 for about 185 miles (300km) toward Florence (or, as the Italians call it, Firenza), and then continue on to either Bologna or Modena, both of which lie within easy reach of Maranello, the home of Ferrari. At which point, I'd give the lovely Nina a call and see about meeting up in Stuttgart, where I planned to stay until I was no longer welcome.

If you are travelling north from the Italian capital, Maranello is really very simple to find; it sits about 30 miles (50km) west of Bologna, amid some lovely scenery and is arrived at via some cracking roads. You can take the E45 towards Modena for a quick run, then peel off along the SS12, or, if you have the time, take the scenic route.

The journey up toward Florence/Firenza involved a great deal of dull motorway slog, and while the SV's tank range is pretty good, my tolerance to such journeys isn't. Frustrated, tired and saddle-sore, I decided to stop and grab a coffee; it was then that an annoying thing happened. In my catatonic state I must have forgotten to put the side-stand down on my bike before getting off: a simple mistake which resulted in the best part of 200 kilograms (440lb) of bike and luggage crashing down on me and pinning me to the ground beneath it. Thankfully, my Sidi boots did their job and prevented my ankle from snapping like a twig, but at that time, trapped under my bike and with petrol beginning to spill out all over the place, I was in no mood to be thankful for small mercies. I was in need of help, but despite the obvious gravitas of my situation, it was slow in coming.

Give yourself a few extra days and stay off the motorways; it's worth it.

In hindsight, were I to have witnessed the spectacle from the perspective of the three chaps opposite me, I'm sure I too, would have seen the humour in it, though I hope I would have managed to stop laughing at least long enough to be of some assistance. When it became clear that they weren't about to rush to my aid of their own accord I began appealing for help in the best Italian I could manage, given the circumstances. Unfortunately, this seemed to translate as: "Don't worry about me. You just chat amongst yourselves for a bit; I'm fine here underneath this motorbike."

Finally, and with a frankly staggering lack of urgency, they decided to cautiously remove the bike and see what this strange foreigner might do next by way of entertainment. What I did next will remain undocumented, save to say it involved very little in the way of gratitude ...

The nearest campsite to Firenza I could find turned out to be some 18 miles (30km) further north, near the village of Maresca, about 12 miles (20km) from Pistoia, and the journey there, along empty, winding roads, afforded some of the most idyllic scenery I'd seen since the Route Napoleon. Lush green hills roll away as far as the eye can see, dotted here and there with charming white houses and picturesque little farms. No wonder Enzo Ferrari refused to leave his beloved homeland.

At 1200 meters (3900 feet) above sea level, the Campsite Foresta del Teso – appropriately situated in the midst of the Foresta del Teso – is a quiet and lonesome place, and the perfect antidote to the hustle and bustle of Rome. The website will proudly inform you that the campsite has 'modern and efficient bathrooms and toilets' and I certainly wouldn't disagree. However, for many, myself included, the stunning scenery – rather than the efficient loos – is the site's

Like Wales without the rain. The stunning Italian countryside.

main attraction. High up in the mountains, the brisk air was altogether different to the grime-ridden pollution I'd been inhaling for the past 48 hours.

After unpacking and setting up my tent, I decided to go for a stroll in the woods, which went on a bit longer than I'd planned. In fact, it was dark when I got back to the campsite, and there wasn't a soul around. I checked on the Suzuki then headed back to my tent which, illuminated by the pale moonlight, more closely resembled an outside larder for one of the caravans parked nearby. It really was stupidly small; in my haste to escape London I'd grabbed the first tent I'd seen that looked like it would fit on the back of a motorbike, without a thought for comfort or practically. As a result, each

night felt like a surreal Alice in Wonderland adventure and, with the exception of a few hotel beds, I don't think I was able to lay down straight for an entire month. Hunched up in my tent, I also felt a chill in the air for the first time since leaving England. Presumably, the altitude of the campsite had a lot to do with this, but still, it was an unpleasant reminder that I was leaving the Mediterranean coast behind.

I pulled on a couple more T-shirts and my bike gloves and lay there shivering in the darkness, cursing my lack of preparation. In addition to buying a tent designed for children, I'd also not packed any warm clothes to speak off, essentially because I'd read 'France' and 'Italy' on my map and assumed it would be baking hot. And it was

My home for a month, dwarfed by a plastic table and chairs.

– in the day. At night, up in the mountains it was tantamount to freezing. I learnt a valuable lesson on that trip: no matter how little storage space you have, and no matter how hot you expect to be, always pack a jumper and some woollen socks.

These days, I use Oxford Sports panniers, which, despite being something of a pain in the arse to fit to your bike each morning, are pretty roomy and allow you to go a little overboard on the 'essentials' list. However, on this trip, all my belongings were bundled into a Gearsack tailpack, which I'd bought cheap from a man in a car park in East Dulwich who was using it to carry potatoes. To be fair, it performed pretty well, despite being far too small for my needs.

Good quality, waterproof luggage is a must for any long journey, but knowing what to pack is equally important. You'll need to be ready for any eventually, so focus on the important stuff. Don't, for example, pack a suit. I don't know what I was thinking, but as it turned out, not once during my trip was I required to slip into the Armani two-piece and act all James Bond. I did, of course, need insect repellent, sun block and thermal clothing, all of which I'd vetoed because I'd decided that at some point I'd want to visit a casino! I also didn't pack a knife, fork, can opener, bottle opener, corkscrew or a medical kit (but I did have four toilet rolls and a huge Lonely Planet guide, which left me with just enough space for a bow tie).

11

Houses of the Holy

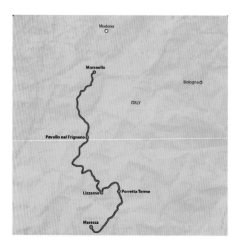

20th August

The grass was wet with dew when I crawled out of my tent the next morning, and I packed quickly, keen to push on to Maranello and see those famous factory gates. In fact, I got up so early that I found myself alone in the campsite, wondering when and if the manager, who held the keys to the car park, would finally stir.

To kill time I checked over the Suzuki, doing the usual pre-ride ritual which involved checking the oil (didn't need topping up once in over 4000 miles (6500km)), the coolant (similar), the lights and tyre pressures and the chain, which, thanks to my Scottoiler, remained well-lubricated and cleaner than me for the most part.

A great-looking bike.

With the SV in near-showroom condition, I returned to the task of trying to escape the car park. After ten minutes or so of politely ringing the bell at reception, I took to stomping around and bumping into chairs and tables, hopeful that the fear of burglary would prompt the manager into action. When this, too, proved futile, I decided to warm up my bike for a while. Sure enough, the crack and burble of the V-twin shattered the early morning silence, and within seconds a blurry-eyed fellow holding a set of keys came stumbling out of his cabin, pyjamas trailing in the mud.

Perfect solitude: just me, the bike and mile after mile of empty road.

Parked up on the outskirts of heaven.

I apologised (in)sincerely for disturbing him and paid my bill, feeling a tiny bit guilty but sure this would pass as the day wore on. By way of an apology I decided to turn off the engine and freewheel down the hill; en route, I stopped to ask directions from two early morning ramblers who seemed grateful that at least one biker had the decency to keep the noise down at that time of day. However, my enquiry as regards directions had the unfortunate effect of triggering a blazing row between the two aged locals, neither of whom (as far as I could tell) had ever heard of Maranello, although each insisted the other's directions were wrong. I had never seen such wild gesticulation and undiluted passion. Each stabbed at what seemed to be random roads on my map, pointing furiously at unpronounceable towns whilst simultaneously showing astonishment at the other's ignorance. Just when it seemed an agreement was about to be reached, another

fellow arrived and, without even knowing where I was going, dismissed the truce out of hand and the debate flared up once again.

I'm sure these three gents would have argued to the grave had a maternal-looking lady not then turned up, and carefully explained that I needed to take the SP632 until it joined the SS64 near Porretta Terme, and then the SP324 to Lizzano in Belvedere, after which I should carry on to Pianone, continuing along the SP324 until it divided into the SP30. After a series of exciting switchbacks, the SP30 becomes the SS12. Heading northward towards Pavullo nel Frignano, the SS12 eventually divides, allowing you to take the SP3 the rest of the way to Maranello. It sounds convoluted and it is, but the roads are great and it's worth the effort compared to the far simpler A1 route noted earlier if you have the time.

Despite the relatively short distance from Pistoia to Maranello (about 60

The famous church in the middle of Maranello, the bells of which are said to chime every time a Ferrari wins a Grand Prix.

miles/100km), the serpentine roads, combined with the stunning scenery, meant that the journey took the best part of three hours, during which time the sun gradually retreated to make way for some ominous-looking clouds. Riding in the rain is no fun at all, but thankfully, just as I'd decided to pull over and change into my waterproofs, I noticed up ahead a small, unobtrusive little signpost, partially hidden by bushes, which quietly welcomed me to Maranello – home of Ferrari.

I'm not sure what I was expecting, but I'll admit to being a tad disappointed as I made by way through the town centre. Maranello could easily be mistaken for any number of small industrial towns dotted across Europe. It's not until you start down the Via Abetone Inferiore, travel about 300 yards (270 metres), and suddenly find yourself right outside the gates of the Ferrari

factory that the true majesty of the place hits you.

The red brick building with the big yellow Ferrari sign across the façade will send shivers down the spine of any true motor racing fan. The history and the glamour; the famous racers who have passed through those hallowed gates: Villeneuve, Schumacher, Fangio, Collins, Alonso and countless others, many of whom gave their lives for the glory of the Scuderia. For the non-motor racing fan, the best analogy I can make is with Willie Wonka's Chocolate Factory (bear with me): behind closed doors miracles are performed by men and women who seem untouchable and charmed. And every so often a little piece of magic will emerge to fuel the fantasy that bit more.

The Scuderia Ferrari (which translates as the Ferrari stable) has been based in this quiet little town since 1943, when Enzo

Outside the gates of the Ferrari factory: note strict adherence to dress code.

Ferrari (already a successful racer for Alfa Romeo) relocated from nearby Modena, and began manufacturing racing cars. Ferrari's dominance of motor racing really took off in the 1950s, when the Formula One World Championship was created and the team began to exert itself: Alberto Ascari won for the Scuderia in '52 and '53, Juan Manuel Fangio in '56, and Mike Hawthorn in '58.

But Ferrari didn't just excel in Formula One; over the years its sports car division has created some of the most evocative and successful machines ever to be raced, and secured prestigious wins in such legendary events as the Mille Miglia, the Targa Floria, and the Le Mans 24 Hours race (which was won by a Ferrari every year from 1960 to 1965).

Known affectionately and reverentially as The Old Man, Enzo Ferrari was a hard, tragic figure whose life was shadowed by grief and death. Not only did some of Italy's

most famous sportsmen perish in his cars, but his closest relatives also died long before their time: the First World War claimed the lives of his father and older brother, while Enzo lost his beloved son, Alfredo 'Dino,' tragically young, from which he never truly recovered. The Old Man would visit his son's grave every day for the rest of his life, quietly reminiscing in the early morning sunshine.

Of the motor racing heroes who have driven under the banner of the Prancing Horse, one name stands out above all others: Gilles Villeneuve, a French Canadian whom Enzo adored like a son. Gilles was one of the greatest talents ever to sit behind the wheel of a racing car, and was affectionately christened the 'High Priest of Destruction' by Enzo, owing to his ability to stress every component of his car to, and often beyond, its limits. Tenacious and brave in equal measure, Gilles' superhuman abilities endeared him to race fans the world over, and for good

One of the stable's greatest: the 250 GTO, pictured in the (now defunct) Nürburgring museum.

reason: 11 seconds faster than anyone else in the rain at Watkins Glen in '79; winning in Spain in '81, despite his ill-handling Ferrari; the astonishing battle with Arnoux at Dijon, also in '79 – still considered by many to be the finest five laps in the history of the sport.

Villeneuve was killed during qualifying for the 1982 Belgian Grand Prix in a crash that would finally bring to a close a series of events that have since passed into motor racing folklore. During the previous Grand Prix at Imola in Italy, Villeneuve and his team-mate, French driver Didier Pironi, had neared the end of the race in first

and second places respectively. Ferrari had long adhered to a system whereby once its cars were first and second on the track, the inter-team battle would end and the leading driver would take the victory: no point risking all in a rash, last-gasp overtake that may result in disaster – it was after all, the team which mattered above all else. So it was that entering the last lap, and with fuel levels critical, the team had shown its drivers the 'Slow' sign – ease off, protect the car, the fight is over. Gilles did so, but Pironi had other ideas: he passed Villeneuve and took the lead, winning the race and leaving

The Ristorante Cavallino: where the chosen few come to dine.

desperate to even the score, yet it was Pironi who was fractionally ahead as qualifying neared its conclusion. Villeneuve, his tyres shot, had no choice but to accept defeat and resume the battle the following day. The team signalled him to return to the pits, but he never made it. Exiting a left-hand kink before the Terlamenbocht corner at 225khp (140mph), Villeneuve ploughed into the back of the March being driven by Jochan Mass. The Ferrari became airborne, then slammed back down onto the circuit, hurling Gilles' body from the wreckage before careering across the track in a series of horrific cartwheels. Villeneuve died in hospital later that day.

his team-mate incensed at what he saw as Pironi's treachery.

At the next race, held at Belgium's uninspiring Zolder circuit, Villeneuve was

Like everyone who knew Gilles, Enzo was devastated by the loss. Once again, the machines that bore his name had brought pain and sadness to the Old Man's doorstep.

Fiorano: Ferrari's private test track, sadly, not in use at the time of my visit.

Oh to be a fly on that particular (tyre) wall.

Enzo Ferrari died on 14 August 1988, less than a month before Gerhard Berger and Jean Alesi secured an emotional one/two victory in the Italian Grand Prix at Monza – the team's first and only win of the season.

It's romance and tragedy such as this which fuels the Ferrari legend and inspires the devotion of the Tifosi – the hardcore Ferrari fan-base that descends like a scarlet mist at racetracks the world over. No other team delivers the same quota of triumph and despair as Ferrari; neither do they polarise opinion like the Maranello squad. Being a Ferrari fan is not always a popular choice, especially in England where the partisan press regularly cry 'cheat' when the Italians come out on top. But at the end of the day, you are what you are.

Opposite the factory and next to the Ristorante Cavallino – which has long been the eatery of choice for the mechanics and drivers who work over the road – is a dedicated Ferrari store that is certainly worth a visit, but around the corner (follow the road to the right of the store) there's a much smaller shop that sells everything the casual tourist could want, and doesn't charge 300 euros (£250/$390) for a keyring.

If you turn left out of the large Ferrari store, back on to Via Abetone Inferiore, after a couple of hundred metres you'll come to a small roundabout where, if you turn right, you'll find a street called Viale Alfredo Dino Ferrari. Head along it and you'll come to an excellent Ferrari museum/gallery; carry on to the end of the road and

Right, where do I sleep?

you'll be at Fiorano, Ferrari's official test track.

If you're lucky, the boys in red will be putting their latest creation through its paces, and you can watch free of charge through the thin catch fencing. Unfortunately, the place was silent and deserted when I visited, but like standing at the gates of the factory, there was something magical and captivating about it anyway: the drivers and cars that have tested there, hour after hour, day after day, in search of those elusive tenths of a second that make the difference between triumph and despair.

At this point I should probably apologise to those readers who neither understand nor share my enthusiasm for deserted bits of road behind catch fences. But, like a football fan standing on the turf at an empty Wembley stadium, or a tennis fan at Wimbledon, it's the memory of what has been and the tacit hint of what will follow that lends such places their sombre majesty. I would experience an identical feeling later that day when I visited the Imola racetrack, 60 or so miles (100km) east of Maranello: the emptiness, the silence, the serenity of a sleeping giant. I rode away from Maranello with the same feeling one gets as a child when the summer holidays are almost at an end.

Count Francesco Baracca stands next to his plane, which bears the now famous image of the Prancing Horse.

Ferrari and Porsche are two of the great motorsport rivals. They've been battling each other on the track for decades and, while Porsche has never threatened its Italian rival in the world of Formula One, its sports cars have given the Maranello squad more than a few headaches over the years. Interestingly, however, due to a remarkable series of events, the companies' logos may share a common heritage.

As any Tifosi will tell you, Ferrari took its logo from the insignia of an Italian First World War fighter ace, Count Francesco Baracca. Baracca had been killed in action, and the story goes that the Count's mother offered Enzo Ferrari her son's insignia following Ferrari's victory at a race in Ravenna.

The animal at the centre of the Porsche logo is taken from the coat-of-arms of Stuttgart, Porsche's home city, which depicts a horse, rearing against a yellow background. It's uncannily similar to the image on the side of Baracca's plane – the one ultimately adopted by Ferrari – and potentially for very good reason. It has been suggested, notably by journalist and historian Giovanni Lurani, that after downing a German plane, Baracca adopted the pilot's emblem as a mark of respect for a particularly worthy rival.

It's tempting to believe that the downed pilot was of Stuttgart origin and therefore flying his city's coat-of-arms. If Barraca indeed adopted this crest, it means that through an extraordinary twist of fate, Porsche and Ferrari are both displaying the same equine image on the badges that grace their cars, but for entirely different reasons.

12

Time for heroes

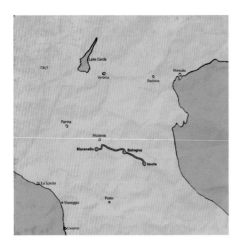

From Maranello it should have been so easy to reach Imola. A virtual straight line along the E45; just continue on through and past Bologna, carry on, don't deviate ... However, on this occasion, I refuse to shoulder any blame for getting lost, with the possible exception of being stupid enough to pay attention to the idiotic signposts when I should have simply ignored them and followed my instincts. At one point I came across a roundabout with three exits: the one I was joining from and the other two heading off at 45 degrees from one another; the signpost for Imola pointed directly in-between them both.

Perhaps the artist who made up that sign felt that, aesthetically, it was more pleasing that the directions point the way they did, rather than follow the crass pragmatism of the Tarmac. I should imagine he was a temperamental sort who, when confronted with those beastly, utilitarian roads, shuddered and fumed at their lack of beauty. No doubt, after completing his masterpiece, he left strict instructions with the local council to rebuild the roads using his signposts as a template, but politics and art rarely fuse and thus the sorry, bungling roads were forced to co-exist with the haughty, petulant road sign for evermore, leaving the traveller in a right mess.

By the time I reached the outskirts of Imola I had very few good words left to say about Italy. Still, I determined to push on and eventually found myself amid the grounds of a tranquil park, nestled within which lay the Imola racetrack. I was here to visit the memorial to Ayrton Senna, who lost his life on 1 May 1994 at the fast, sweeping, left-hand corner named Tamburello.

When not heaving with race fans, the Imola Park is a beautiful and relaxing place to spend an hour or two, and the perfect location for a memorial to one of the sport's most naturally gifted, intelligent and focussed drivers. The bronze statue of Senna, which stands near the corner where he died, is a sombre, pensive affair that well captures his thoughtful, emotional character. It's a moving tribute and I was glad I took the time to visit it.

Imola, like Hockenheim before it, has become a synonym for tragedy and loss.

A tribute to Enzo: this five metre tall collection of F40s by French sculptor Arman sits outside the gates of the Autodromo Internazionale Enzo e Dino Ferrari (Imola).

A poignant and fitting tribute to one of the greats ...

... Senna.

I decided to find a campsite in Imola (the town, not the racing circuit), which, as it turns out is like trying to find a needle in a haystack; furthermore, the signposts hinting at the direction of the needle had clearly been erected by someone keen to ensure that

that particular object remained hidden for all time. Eventually, I stopped riding round in circles long enough to ask a policeman for help, who informed me that there was neither a needle, a haystack nor a campsite in the whole of Imola, and I should head back toward Bologna if I wanted to find a place to sleep. I followed his advice and, after a torturous journey through rush hour traffic, managed to find a campsite where I erected my tent just before it began to rain.

I sat under the canvas for a while, updating my notes, listening to the pitter-patter of the rain, and wondering what on earth I was going to do for the rest of the evening. The campsite was effectively in the middle of nowhere, which left me with no option other than to go to the site bar and stay there until it closed. Begrudgingly I accepted my fate, but en route I was intercepted by an English couple who wanted directions to somewhere or other I hadn't heard of. I explained that of all the people in the campsite, and quite possibly Italy, I was the last person they should seek advice from as regards directions. By way of elaboration, I provided a brief overview of the day's struggle across 30 miles (50km) of straight Italian motorway, after which they accepted my refusal to even look at their map as an act of great kindness. We decided to seek advice elsewhere and headed off to the bar as one.

It turned out that John and Julie had given up their London jobs to make the trip of a lifetime from London to Australia … in a Land Rover. They planned to see the world and bolster the coffers of some charity or other in the process; given the appearance of their vehicle they were obviously serious about the journey. It looked like something the marines would use to stage a beach invasion: the roof was covered in spotlights and petrol canisters, while the entire front of the thing was hidden behind a massive bull bar. The windows were made from some special reinforced glass and the tires were technically unburstable.

It seemed excessive, until I realised how ill-prepared its occupants were for what lay instore. Julie, for example, said in all seriousness that, should the worst come to the worst, they would be prepared to tough it out in the back of their Land Rover for a night or two, on the off-chance that they couldn't find anywhere more comfortable to stay. I've never been to Cambodia, but from what I've heard, the back of a Land Rover would qualify as five star accommodation in many parts of the country. She also kept going on about being a vegetarian and how she thought she may struggle to find a decent meal in India and Thailand. India and Thailand! Good grief, I'd nearly starved trying to find a cheese sandwich in France.

It's strange how it's only through the suffering of others that we're prepared to open our wallets for charity. If those two had been driving down from Sheffield to Nice in a Bentley Continental they wouldn't have secured enough sponsorship for the petrol money. But tell your friends and relatives you are going to put yourself through hell for the next six months and they'll hurl cash at you without a second thought. There is a reasonable possibility that those two folk may have met some gruesome fate on that journey, but I doubt that crossed the minds of those sponsoring them; it only mattered that they endure some degree of discomfort to justify the odd donation. Surely it would make more sense to reverse the process? To say: "Look here, father, if you don't give £200 to Oxfam, I shall bungee jump off London Bridge and probably die."

After a while it became clear that John and Julie were hoping I'd offer some kind of sponsorship myself, whilst I was doing my best to extract another beer from them: we all went to bed disappointed.

13

You show me yours (and I'll show you mine)

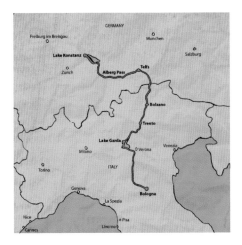

21st August

The next morning I packed quickly and was on the road by 8am. I'd spoken to Nina, who wasn't quite as pleased to hear from me as I'd anticipated – possibly because in my enthusiasm to make contact I'd called her at about quarter to seven in the morning. Anyway, we'd agreed that I'd stop by her place in Stuttgart the following Tuesday, which seemed great news until I paused to consider the journey. Stuttgart is about 470 miles (750km) from Bologna, and to get there you must cross the Alps. From my maps, I couldn't determine anything like a straight or simple route, and suddenly the Tuesday deadline seemed hopeful at best, hence my rapid departure from the campsite.

By 9am I was well on my way to Verona, my first checkpoint on a hastily improvised route that would take me through Trento and Bolzano, up and over the Alps, and on to Innsbruck in Austria. I planned on finding a campsite nearby, and then pushing on toward Stuttgart the following day, with a view to arriving that evening or the following morning. I figured the whole journey should take no more than two days and, with the exception of crossing the Alps – which I was a little anxious about – it seemed feasible.

Even so, I'd need to be a little more disciplined about my comfort stops – ie, getting off the bike for nothing other than fuel or food – so I decided to head on through Verona without stopping to experience what I'd heard was its appreciable beauty. To be honest, after Rome and its endless artefacts I felt less inclined to spend hours wandering though ancient monuments or gazing at artistic relics. Instead, I detoured round Lake Garda, which I'd heard was equally stunning, without the obligation to gaze appreciably at things I didn't understand.

Lake Garda is the largest lake in Italy and achingly beautiful. It's surrounded by great roads, and would make a perfect destination for a motorcycle holiday in itself. For some reason, I'd expected Garda to resemble Lake Coniston in the English Lake District; a kind of maudlin retreat for Ted Hughes* devotees keen to wallow in the mournful

*According to Mike, who proofed the manuscript for me, Coniston is the wrong side of the Penines for Hughes; apparently, Wordsworth and Southey (and Bragg) would have been more appropriate examples … he's still livid about the tent fiasco.

91

The affluent and beautiful Lake Garda. A fine place to relax and enjoy the waves.

sobriety of an aged natural wilderness. Lake Garda is more like a Florida waterpark without the Americans. Actually, that's a bit harsh. What I mean is that it's bright and cheerful and sunny and rich, populated by tanned, relaxed and affluent-looking middle aged couples watching their offspring water-ski and play on expensive-looking boats.

I found a restaurant by the side of the lake and sat watching the world go by, eating pizza and recapping on the journey so far.

When I left London I literally had no idea where I was going, let alone what I might find; I just wanted to get away, to feel the sun on my face without it first passing through an office window. Yes, I was worried about crashing or getting massively lost, but I was more afraid that I'd bottle it after a

couple of days and return home, humbled and humiliated. But here I was, three weeks in and going strong, having ridden all the way to Rome and survived foreign campsites, French toilets, Italian signposts, tidal waves, a grilling by the police, and plenty of other fairly trivial instances that I could embellish into thrilling tales upon my return. It struck me that perhaps I should write a book …

With thoughts of chat show appearances and a Pulitzer firmly in mind, I waved goodbye to Lake Garda and its enviable residents and pushed on toward the Alps, finally reaching Bolzano, near the Italo-Austrian border, late in the afternoon. Despite the pressing Stuttgart deadline, I'd been unable to resist taking the slower, though much more enjoyable, scenic route from Lake Garda,

Another rest break, another picture of the Suzuki. This time on the shores of Lake Garda.

bypassing the quick and simple A22 in favour of the frankly stunning Parco naturale provinciale dell' Adamello Brenta.

Like a miniature Grenoble, Bolzano is entirely surrounded by vast mountains that give the place a Tolkienian atmosphere; an impression reinforced by the vicious little goblin at the campsite reception desk. About 16 years old and precocious with it, she was clearly labouring there at the behest of her parents and had determined to get her own back by driving away all the customers.

"Huh?" she grunted, by way of a greeting, as I stood at the counter trying to work out if I was still in Italy or if I'd crossed the border into Austria (and therefore what language to say hello in). I decided to play it safe and used neither.

"Hello," I said in plain English. "Am I in Austria?"

I don't know whether she understood me or not; her look of bemused contempt could have applied either way.

I repeated my question and, to help her out, I raised my voice a little:

"Excuse me, could you tell me what country I'm in please?"

She gave an exaggerated sigh and glanced up at the heavens. I was impressed: this young girl, no more than 15 years of age, had already achieved a far more efficient means of communication than the clumsy spoken word. With growing agitation I turned and made a sweeping gesture that clearly translated as: "This land you see before you, girl, I demand to know its name."

She squinted at me, as if unable to determine what strange species she was dealing with.

With little hope, I pointed to the outside world and meekly enquired:

"Is this Italy?"

She shrugged and walked away.

Still none the wiser, I turned and walked straight into the site manager, who was moderately less dismissive than his offspring, and who wearily checked me in for the night. He explained that I was still just about in Italy and asked – unnecessarily to my mind – whether I knew where I'd come from? I said London via Rome and he looked confused.

Next to my patch of sun-dried grass was a group of sexagenarians from, I think,

Denmark: the men were drinking beer and polishing their ancient, though lovingly restored, Nimbus motorbikes, which had sidecars attached for their wives to ride in. These looked extremely uncomfortable, with no discernible suspension to speak of (the motorbikes, I mean, not the wives), but the old machines seemed to be holding up well.

Noticing my interest, one of the group ambled over and began pointing to various bits of my Suzuki, keen to demonstrate how things had changed in the millennium or so since his bike had been built. We stood staring appreciably at each other's machines as the realisation dawned that neither of us could speak the other's language. It was an awkward few minutes; I blurted out things like 'fast' and 'twin' in unnecessarily loud

Awkward moment in Bolzano.

English while the old fellow tried to reply in the only English he knew, which turned out to be the numbers 1 to 10. Thus, we embarked on a painfully stunted chat that revolved solely around the engine size of our respective bikes.

"650"

"65?"

"No, six hundred and fifty"

"Sixty??"

"Swiss?"

"What?"

"Nine?"

"No mine"

"25?"

And so it went on until we were both so confused that we just stood there smiling uneasily for about 40 seconds. Finally, I pushed a can of lager into his hand, thanked him for nothing in particular and retreated at a slight jog to my tent.

22nd August

The next morning I got up early, keen to avoid another numerical exchange with my neighbours. Having packed and paid in record time, I soon found myself hurling the Suzuki through the wonderful Alpine scenery. I'm not entirely sure which roads I travelled along, but after an hour or so I arrived at a little town called Telfs which sits just west of Innsbruck. Telfs is a charming place in a *Sound of Music* sort of a way, but I fear any further attempt to describe its quaint, tranquil qualities would make it sound utterly dull, so I'll just say it's very

Telfs (I think). To be fair, a lot of these places look the same. All very peaceful and pretty with a quite spectacular backdrop.

pretty and its pleasant market community is friendly and sells nice fruit.

From Telfs, I began my ascent of the Alps (well, a bit of them) via the Arlberg Pass, stopping every few kilometres to breathe in the crisp, pure air and admire the tremendous views. I'd anticipated freezing, snow-covered highways and roaring blizzards, but in reality the roads were clear and smooth, the sun shone brightly in the cloudless sky, and the entire Alpine experience turned out to be one of the most enjoyable of the journey. In hindsight I wish I'd spent days, rather than hours, amid that rugged and beautiful scenery. Parked at the side of the road, gazing out across the mountains, it was wonderfully peaceful, with nothing but a light breeze caressing my face and a long, empty winding road stretching off into the distance: the only indication I wasn't completely alone in the world.

Alpine roads demand a certain respect; not only because they are twisty and awkward and often flanked with menacing drops measured in hundreds of feet, but also because if you do throw your bike down the road and hurt yourself, you're unlikely to be found for a while (if at all). I rode along those treacherous mountain paths with fear as my pillion. I couldn't shake the notion that the smallest mistake might end with me either plummeting to my death or lying in a heap at the bottom of a frozen ditch, totally obscured from the view of other road users and utterly helpless.

So I tempered my pace, tried to relax, and put my faith in the Suzuki's versatile suspension. Eventually, the road stopped going up and began to descend, gently at first, and then with unexpected severity. It's surprising how much physical effort is involved in riding a heavy bike downhill continuously for the best part of 90 minutes; under braking – which happens quite a lot – your forearms and wrists take the full weight of your upper body, including, in my case, a rucksack which was full to bursting. It's like doing countless push-ups while also trying to concentrate on the road ahead, noting and avoiding that innocuous-looking patch of gravel that could so easily rob the front tyre of its grip, or the pothole ready to hammer your already fully compressed suspension and send a bone-shaking jolt through the bars and down your spine. By the time I got to the bottom of the pass I was exhausted.

But the effort had been worth it: those magnificent views are one of the abiding memories of my trip, and perhaps my only regret is that I didn't spend more time up in the mountains. I don't think I've experienced an environment before or since that is at once so awe-inspiring, intimidating and incredibly beautiful.

Still, I took comfort from the fact that the Alps were unlikely to go anywhere soon and determined to return when I had more time and a less attractive deadline to meet. As it was, I decided to push on for another 30 miles (50km) or so until I reached the shores of Lake Konstanz, a beautiful and popular tourist resort just a couple of hours' ride from Stuttgart.

Konstanz is a huge body of water (55 billion cubic metres worth!) plummeting down 252 metres (275 yards) at its deepest point. But such prosaic facts were far from my mind as I settled down outside my tent with a bottle of German beer in my hand and the foreboding Alps away to my left, shrouded in mist. The sun was setting to my right, its furious reflection a shimmering pathway stretching out across the massive lake, whose waves lapped against the shore as the silhouettes of distant boats rocked gently on the horizon. And ducks! Flapping and quacking and dithering to and fro. It's a lazy place, that lake; tinged with an air of melancholy as day succumbs to night's embrace.

Brits abroad: Rich and Tracey were enjoying a similar trip to mine, albeit on a slightly more comfortable bike.

14

Achtung, baby

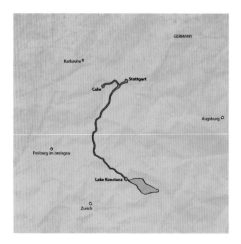

23rd August

What a rotten place Lake Konstanz turned out to be. It rained on and off all night long, and its proximity to the Alps, coupled with the breeze from the lake, made the tent cold and uncomfortable. I awoke to discover all my possessions damp from the heavy dew, including my phone, which was ruined. Still, I would happily have remained in my cosy sleeping bag a while longer were it not for the terrible English family that had set up camp next to me. They seemed intent on waking the entire site with their clanging and crying and shouting to one another as they went about their early morning routine, which seemed to consist of one of the children

being told to perform some rudimentary task – fetching water for the stove or finding a clean cup – while the other child did its level best to murder him.

Finally, there came a moment of calm and I stole the opportunity to creep out of my tent and see if the storm had passed. All being quiet, I was about to pack up and depart when I discovered that this loathsome family had used my bike as a clothes horse! My pride and joy, a mass of towels and socks and underwear. I strode over to the father of the family and pointed to the crime scene; he laughed pleasantly and asked if I would like him to remove the offending items. During the ensuing chat he stopped laughing and began to look sad, then afraid. I think I can safely say I earned my place in heaven that morning. No-one died.

With the offending items removed from the Suzuki, I loaded her up and began the 155 mile (250km) ride to Stuttgart, which I hoped wouldn't take more than a couple of hours. The sky looked awfully black as I set off and I feared the worst. Unfortunately, the worst did not fear me and within minutes of leaving the campsite the heavens opened and did not close for the next three hours, when I pulled into a service station and cursed the very notion of motorcycling. Finally, when it became clear the rain wasn't going to stop or even ease any time soon, I plunged back into the monsoon and eventually found Nina's house at around one that afternoon, four-and-half hours after leaving Konstanz.

I'd envisaged my arrival at Nina's as being like that carnival scene from *Ferris Bueller's Day Off* – an heroic occasion with wild celebrations, ticker tape raining down and jubilant applause from gathered neighbours. It wasn't. Far from conveying the impression of heroic traveller, my bedraggled appearance was more suggestive of a drowned rat. Nina looked me up and down cautiously, as though I was not quite what she had been expecting. She gingerly hugged me, then stepped back and, wiping herself, suggested that perhaps I would like to go inside and get changed. I thought I detected something akin to disappointment in her voice, although I may have been mistaken; it might have been disgust.

Thankfully, I was treated to the most wonderful hospitality by Nina's family, and within minutes of arriving I found myself enjoying a luxurious bath while my clothes dried by the fireplace. To be honest, they could have locked me in the garden shed with a cigarette lighter and a soiled blanket and I'd have been grateful, but no effort was spared – at least on the part of Nina's parents – to make my stay as pleasant as possible.

Later that afternoon we took a stroll around Stuttgart (the rain stopped the moment I reached the house), during which Nina proudly pointed out some famous buildings while I made suitably impressed

Stuttgart, the German Sheffield. (Courtesy Stuttgart Marketing GmbH)

noises and wondered how long the tour would last.

That's not to suggest that Stuttgart is anything other than a lovely place, and I'm sure its residents have every reason to be proud of their city. We passed a castle of sorts and something that resembled a library, then sat for a while next to a large thing in the city centre; this was followed by a ride in a lift up something quite high, before not seeing what we'd come to see and going back down again. Then we walked past some building or other that somebody I should have known but didn't had worked in, before taking a trip through a market that seemed like any other in Europe but was actually over a million years old. And then, thank goodness, I spied Nina's car and knew I was saved.

In fact, I doubt Stuttgart is any less interesting than most moderately-sized European cities, but in this instance it was having to compete with the likes of Rome, Monte Carlo and Grenoble, which is a tall order in anyone's book. However, in its defence, I can say it is both clean and tidy, and surrounded by a lovely park.

In fact, what struck me most about Stuttgart was its similarity to Sheffield, a city I know reasonably well having spent three years there at university, and then another two engaged in some of the most dreadful jobs known to mankind. It shares with its German counterpart a fairly spacious central shopping area, as well as an enviable proximity to vast amounts of countryside and parkland. In Stuttgart it is the Black Forest that provides this much-needed counterpoint; in Sheffield, the Peak District.

I should imagine the most prominent memory that anyone who has ever lived in Sheffield has of the place is its hilly geography, which makes travelling anywhere a mammoth task, particularly in winter when heavy snowfall is common.

One particularly unpleasant journey springs to mind. Returning home from work on a dark, snowy, winter's evening, I became trapped halfway down a hill near the busy Ecclesall Road. I was still driving the Spitfire at the time, not the most practical of vehicles on the best of days, but in such torrid, icy conditions it was frankly lethal. The road suddenly became far too slippery to drive the rest of the way down, so I parked up and hoped that a gritting lorry would pass by at some point before I froze to death.

Then I witnessed a sight I shall never forget – slowly, out of the darkness, as though on skates, glided a brand new Mercedes, at the wheel of which sat a forlorn-looking chap in a rather nice suit. I assume at some point during his descent he'd tried to bring his vehicle to a halt, but by the time he slid past me he'd clearly given up trying. He seemed utterly accepting of his fate; he even managed a little smile as I caught his eye. I remember his face was such a picture of dignified resignation that I felt quite proud to be British. I sat there and watched that man and his expensive car slide all the way down the hill, as did the fellow whom he eventually crashed in to. He was also trapped on the ice and together they made for a rather curious spectacle, but a memorable one, nonetheless.

24th August

Herman Hesse was a German author, most famous for his novels *Das Glasperlenspiel (The Glass Bead Game)* and *Steppenwolf.* As well as being a famous novelist, he was also a prolific painter and poet, and all-round decent chap. I know all this because I visited his house – now a museum in Calw, just outside of Stuttgart – having politely declined a visit to the Mercedes museum which I had wanted to see for years. The conversation which led to this sad state of affairs went something like this:

Admittedly, less like Sheffield in this picture. (Courtesy Stuttgart Marketing GmbH)

Me: So, what will we do today? (let's go to the Mercedes museum)

Nina: Not sure, what would you like to do? (we're not going to that Mercedes museum)

Me: I don't mind, really, perhaps a museum? (I've just ridden 6500 kilometres for this)

Nina: Well, there's that Mercedes place in town, I don't know what it's like. (I know exactly what it's like and I don't want to go there)

Me: Well, maybe we could drive past it and have a look (and stay there for at least four hours)

Nina: Oh, hang on, what about the Herman Hesse museum? It's about an hour away. I've always wanted to visit it. (I've never shown the slightest interest in the place but it beats looking at cars all day)

Me: Who? (you're fucking joking)

(Nina explains who Herman Hesse is)

Me: That sounds interesting (in the 'watching paint dry' sense)

Nina: But you're sure you don't want to visit the Mercedes museum? (because we're not going to, no matter what you say)

Me: No, no, let's drive out into the woods and look at the belongings of someone I've never heard of (how did this happen?)

Nina: Great, I'll make some sandwiches (meat ones – I win)

And so, about three quarters of an hour later, I found myself not gazing appreciatively at Moss' 300 SLR, nor Caracciola's W154, but rather standing in the rain on the outskirts of the Black Forest looking at a map that must have been influenced by the Italian signpost industry.

Still, the journey to Hesse's house was not without its thrills, thanks to the frankly reckless nature of Nina's driving, upon which I felt obliged to comment:

"Careful," I exclaimed as we narrowly avoided a curb.

"That was red," I noted as we sped through a set of traffic lights.

"He'll be alright," I concluded, viewing the maimed figure in the mirror.

My advice, rather than helping, seemed only to infuriate her, but I carried on regardless until she finally exploded; I was tempted to point out that she probably shouldn't have been driving if she couldn't keep her emotions in check, but didn't fancy the walk home.

As it turned out, Hesse was quite an interesting character after all. Born into a privileged family, he had a fairly unhappy childhood by all accounts, getting expelled from one school and detesting the others he attended. At the turn of the twentieth

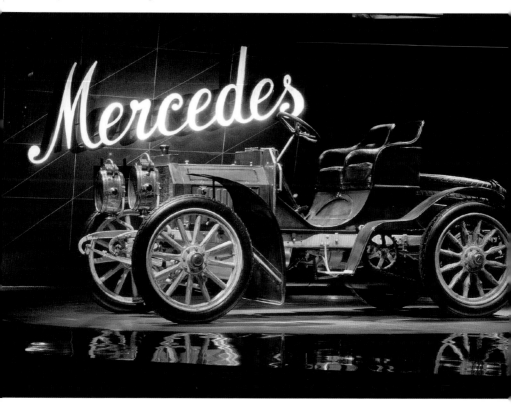

A beautiful old chain-driven Merc. Rarely do you get the chance to see such a wonderful piece of antiquity. Once in a lifetime, perhaps ... (Courtesy Stuttgart Marketing GmbH)

century he began publishing his first works, and gained early critical acclaim with his novel *Peter Camenzind* (I should say at this point that I've never read any of his books and am citing a pamphlet I picked up at the museum as my sole authority on the subject). A trip to India in 1911 saw Hesse catch an early dose of new-age fever and he came back babbling on about the Gautama Buddha, the basis for his book, *Siddhartha*.

The museum guidebook notes – with a pleasingly cavalier approach to melodrama – that, in the years that followed: "Hesse's life continued to be filled with agony." He became an active pacifist during the Second World War and in 1946 was awarded the Nobel Prize for Literature, after which he wrote little and died in his sleep of cerebral haemorrhage on 9 August 1962 at the age of eighty-five.

Hesse's contribution to literature was profound, and his focus on the duality of body and mind, combined with an artistic flair and penchant for fine wine, left an indelible imprint on 20th century culture. Tragically, he is destined to be forever confused with rock giants Steppenwolf, who took their name from Hesse's masterpiece. Maybe he'd have appreciated the irony.

The museum itself was a rather sombre affair, full of pictures of long-dead friends and family members and peppered with hundreds of letters from Hesse, all rather thoughtlessly written in German. Nina translated a few, but she did so with such undisguised reluctance that I decided to leave her to it and went and bought some postcards instead, one of which I'm looking at now. It is black and white and shows Hesse in profile, dressed in a smart suit, reclining on a chair and admiring what must have been a very expensive glass of wine, judging by the satisfied look on his face. He looks a friendly, dignified sort of fellow, and I think I'll stop typing for a while and join him in a glass.

That evening we visited Nina's sister who, without warning, unleashed some horrendous Ben Stiller comedy upon us. The name of the film escapes me but it entailed the tedious courtship of two ostensibly incompatible people who eventually discover that love can blossom between the most unlikely (and unlikable) individuals. I will not pretend that this was how I'd anticipated spending my last night with Nina and will say only that it fell short of expectations.

15

On the road again

25th August

My sojourn in Stuttgart had reached an all too rapid conclusion. Nina and her family were (conveniently) off to visit relatives for a few days, and had declined my offer to house-sit until they returned. Before I left, however, I was treated to a lovely breakfast and when I went outside to load up my bike, I discovered Nina's dad had spent the morning cleaning three weeks worth of dirt and grime from its now pristine fairing. I thanked them all for their kindness, gave Nina as big a kiss as I could get away with, and waved my goodbyes to a nice warm bed and the dream of a new life in Germany.

My next destination was the Ardennes forest, and more specifically Spa

Francorchamps, one of the world's great racetracks, which would shortly be hosting the Belgian Grand Prix.

The journey through Germany was particularly uninteresting, consisting solely of motorways and rain. From Stuttgart there's no easy or direct route to the north-west of the country, so I had to navigate a host of awkward motorway junctions as I first headed toward Karlsruhe, then on to Mannheim, followed by a long and arduous ride through Koblenz and then via Prüm toward Belgium. The route I followed (and there must be an easier one) was about 250 miles (400km) and took most of the afternoon. Finally, however, I found myself in a little town called Büllingen, right on the Belgian-German border. I had planned on heading straight to the circuit, but as it was getting late – and because I wasn't exactly sure where either it or I was – I decided to spend the night in the Hotel International: a grand name for a small hotel run by Marleen and Eddy Van Den Heurck, two of the friendliest people you are ever likely to meet. I was treated to a wonderful supper, accompanied by a healthy selection of fine Belgian beers which it seemed only polite to sample. Unfortunately, my notes become somewhat illegible at this point, but I recall having a very nice evening, although I must have banged my head on my way to bed because it was very sore in the morning.

This is the most interesting image I could find of this section of my journey.

26th August

Spa is just a short 18 mile (30km) hop from Büllingen (follow the N632 which becomes the N62 and takes you to the circuit), and I arrived at the track at around 10am, having pretty much emptied the Hotel International's larder of eggs, toast and coffee.

Arriving at the track mid-morning seemed slightly odd, as for me, Grands Prix are synonymous with ridiculously early starts. I remember when I was young, being cajoled out of bed in the dead of night and hustled into the back of our little Lotus Elan (safety laws weren't what they are now, and as a small child I'd be placed astride the diff housing behind the two front seats). I'd sit there in the dark – slightly bewildered but full of excitement – while my Mom made up a packed lunch and Dad made sure there was film in the camera. Then we'd shoot off down to Brands Hatch or Silverstone, via a host of wrong turns (it's genetic) and eventually find ourselves in some three mile queue of traffic at half past five in the morning, just as the sky was beginning to lighten. By eight we'd be in sight of the entrance and the marshals

would amble over, handing out programmes to inform us which early morning events we were about to miss. Two hours later we'd be encamped on a grass verge down at Woodcote or Copse corner, with a flask of coffee and the decimated remnants of a packet of biscuits, trying to occupy the time before the cars emerged for practice.

Eventually, somewhere in the distance we'd hear the clank of machinery as the pit lane garage doors were hauled open, and a buzz of anticipation would sweep through the crowd. Moments later, an engine would erupt into life, the pistons and valves screaming abuse at the mechanics responsible for waking them. Pretty soon the air would be full of the deafening shriek of those monster V10s being warmed up, the crowd on its feet, desperate to catch a glimpse of the cars and drivers in the paddock. Then finally, that most evocative sound, the screech of the Klaxon which signalled the beginning of practice: one by one the cars would file out onto the track, the crowds cheering with appreciation as a Ligier or Tyrell emerged from the pits, tentative at first, feeling for grip, then, happy with the conditions, picking up speed, faster and faster. Through the complex and on to Hanger Straight, flashing past in an instant; flat out, engines howling before popping and fizzing down through the gears for the right-hander at Stowe. Then a brief moment of calm, followed by something like silence until, slowly at first, but with a spine-tingling inevitability, that indescribable wail would sound in the distance.

The hairs on your neck would stand up as you strained to get a better view; all heads facing right, peering into the morning haze as the cacophony grew louder. Now, almost in sight – the ground actually shaking – a wonderful, deafening white noise that rattled your organs and confounded the senses, and with Dad stabbing the air and shouting "Here they come!" that immense blur of speed would burst from the horizon and head screaming like a banshee straight at you, the engine note spiralling upward until the noise reached its ear-splitting crescendo. Then, in an instant, they'd be gone, the fury disappearing into the distance, just a small cloud of dust lingering in the air, kicked up by an errant wheel pushed wide, beyond the limit.

Witnessing a Formula One car driven in anger is like nothing else in the world; every sense is traumatised by the relentless ferocity as each driver pushes his car to the very limit, and sometimes beyond. Just when you thought it was safe to take your fingers out of your ears another wave of energy would come shrieking past, then another and another, until the whole world gives way to a raging melting pot of crackling engines and roaring crowds. And always a special, throat-grazing cheer for Mansell, the home town hero, 'El Lione' when he drove for Ferrari but always Red Five to me.

Back in the late eighties, when Formula One machines reached their pinnacle in terms of raw power, the tremendous downforce generated by the bodywork and wings would often force the bottom of the car onto the ground, scraping along the asphalt and generating a huge shower of sparks in its wake. And Mansell always had the most sparks. His Williams looked like a 200mph firework as he hurled it through the fast left-right of the complex at Silverstone, balancing the car on the outer limits of adhesion. And every time that little bit faster. Mansell was a frightening driver; once he'd got the bit between his teeth nothing – nothing – would stop him. Unlike Prost or even Senna, he never seemed at ease with his car, always battling and harrying it through every corner, as if convinced it wasn't giving its all, demanding it tried harder, forcing it on with pure determination. That move on

Piquet at Silverstone in '87 was one of the greatest sporting moments of all time.

Anyway, back to Spa. The campsite at the racetrack was not, by any stretch of the imagination, a beautiful place. It had the appearance of a bog with 30,000 cars parked in, rather than on, it. Still, one can't be choosy in such circumstances, and, having put up my tent and bought my ticket, I made my way to the track just as the first cars began exiting the pits. Seated in the grandstand overlooking the daunting Eau Rouge corner – so-called because of the little stream that runs alongside it, coloured red by the iron in the rock – I had what is possibly the best view in motor racing (aside from the cockpit, that is). Formula One cars take Eau Rouge at something like 170mph (270kph), sweeping uphill as the track drifts right, chinking left at the crest, then right again as the track opens out down the long straight towards Les Combes. These days the cars have such incredible levels of grip that the corner is perhaps less of a challenge than it should be, but still every driver shows it a huge amount of respect: you don't have small accidents at Eau Rouge, just ask Jacques Villeneuve.

I spent most of the afternoon in the grandstands, enjoying the action and stuffing myself with doughnuts and coffee. Later on, as dusk began to fall, I went for a stroll around the market area, spending a small fortune on T-shirts and keyrings, before stocking up on crisps and beer and heading back to my tent.

Ever since I'd left Lake Konstanz rain had never been far away, and high up in the Ardennes forest it had been falling on and off all day long. Now it suddenly struck me that I would be spending a rather damp night under canvas, a prospect that didn't appeal in the slightest.

As it transpired, 'rather damp' was an understatement; waterlogged would be

Spa Francorchamps – I'm about to discover that my tent isn't waterproof.

closer to the mark. I should say nothing on land had ever been wetter than that tent. When I unzipped it and discovered my drenched belongings I felt such a wave of sadness that, for a moment, I considered packing up and going home. And I would have done, too, had I not earlier that day paid hundreds of euros for a three-day pass. Much credit must go to my sleeping bag at this point, which, heroically, had tried to save the day by absorbing as much of the water as possible. Without wanting to sound ungrateful, I wished it hadn't bothered.

I sat there in my soggy tent, munching on crisps, drowning my sorrows, and wondering how on earth I would sleep in such abysmal conditions. As it turned out, I need not have worried. The Belgian race fan is not one for sleep. He regards the setting sun as a signal to begin an unrelenting onslaught of fireworks and air horns, accompanied by euro-pop turned up to 11. From nine that evening until at least 4.30 the next morning, there wasn't a moment's lull in the racket.

I can't say I much enjoyed my first night at Spa Francorchamps.

16

The Great Escape

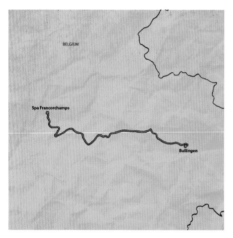

27th August

The next morning, after a hearty thirty minutes' sleep and a cold wash, I joined the ranks of fans heading down to the track to catch the pre-qualifying practice session. Unfortunately for those of us who'd forfeited a lie-in, practice had been delayed due to the low cloud that was preventing the emergency helicopter from taking off. With the helicopter temporarily grounded, the cars would have to wait for the cloud to disappear before practice could begin, so I grabbed a coffee and took up position at La Source – the first, very tight right-hand bend.

As I stood there, reading my sodden programme and trying not to think about how bad the following night would be, I became aware of a presence to my right, and turned to see a scruffy, middle-aged fellow with an untrimmed beard hovering next to me. For a good five minutes he stood there, nodding and smiling and generally being annoying, until I eventually cracked and politely enquired whether he spoke English? As it turned out, not only did he speak English, he couldn't *stop* speaking it. Taking my forced politeness as his cue, he launched into his life story, which transformed the ensuing 50 minutes into a blitzkrieg of quick fire monotony.

Robert, for that was his name, had just turned 50, and had spent most of his life as a chemical engineer manufacturing mustard gas, or something. About five years ago, the thought had struck him that perhaps his chemical arsenal was not, in fact, contributing to global harmony, so he decided to become a carer instead. Indeed, I was left in no doubt as to how much Robert cared, or, for that matter, how undiscriminating he was regarding those things which he cared about. It seemed anything and everything was a potential victim of Robert's ponderous benevolence: from the poor and disabled to the Amazonian rain forests, starving Africans, supermarket monopolies, and the deprived boroughs of south east London, Robert cared about the lot.

Despite my best efforts to stop him, he rambled on about how terrible *this* was and why weren't they doing something about *that* until, finally, I managed to turn the conversation to the Grand Prix, whereupon it became clear he knew absolutely nothing about motor racing. Robert demanded to know why they couldn't just get on with things, and who needed a helicopter for such a short journey anyway? After a while I realised that Robert thought the helicopter would be used only to ferry the doctor to the scene of the accident in the event of an emergency, whereupon the injured driver would be transferred to an ambulance and driven the rest of the way to hospital. Wearily, I pointed out that they would probably remain in the helicopter for the duration of the journey, what with it being about a thousand times faster and all. He looked at me as though I'd just deciphered the Bible code.

"Oh!" he gasped, "yes, well, that would make sense, wouldn't it?"

As it turned out, Robert was on his own that day as the bus-load of race fans he'd arrived with had all mysteriously disappeared the moment his back was turned. I shouted "Look, a helicopter!" and did the same.

Desperate to put some distance between myself and my new friend, I abandoned my favourable viewing spot and trudged up Eau Rouge and halfway down the long Kemmel straight, where I took up a precarious position on a steep, muddy bank overlooking the track. I was surrounded by about a thousand other race fans, most of whom I soon discovered shared a single, irritating trait – it seems the Belgians find a unique hilarity in the spectacle of someone falling over. I concede once, twice even, such a thing is amusing, but after the third, fourth, fifth and six occasions, the humour begins to pale in my opinion, particularly when it happens to be me doing most of the falling.

The first time I slipped down the muddy

Taken during a rare moment when I wasn't tumbling arse over tit.

The drivers' parade: I'd love to see them try and get this round the Loews hairpin.

bank I chuckled along with those imbeciles, keen to show that I also got the joke. The second time, I staggered to my feet and took a bow. The third time, when I happened to be carrying a cheese sandwich and a hot cup of coffee, I merely gave a look which said "I hope you too are able to experience the humour of third-degree burns in the very near future."

Finally, fearing my comic aside was detracting from the main event – and that at some point my painful slapstick would end up on the large TV screens dotted around the track – I decided to relocate, and watched the rest of the day's events in relative safety, although at some distance from the action.

28th August

Thankfully, the following night was not quite the hellish nightmare I'd been anticipating, although that is not to imply it was in any way pleasant. It was cold and damp, but I managed to drown out the racket of innumerable fireworks and klaxons with the help of some new earplugs I'd bought at the track, and thankfully the rain held off. In fact, by the time I took up my trackside position the next day the sun was beaming above and the ground beginning to dry out, which made the prospect of sitting on a grass verge for the next eight hours somewhat more appealing.

Eventually, after what seemed like an eternity, the build-up to the race began. All around the circuit bored, sleepy faces suddenly became alert and focused as the crowd began to buzz with excitement. Mechanics flooded into the pit lane, a mass of coloured overalls scurrying around the cars; now and again a driver appeared, a casual wave to the crowd soliciting a cheer of approval. Loudspeakers around the circuit struggled to convey yesterday's lap times and qualifying positions above the noise of the engines, the commentator's enthusiasm lost amid the fervour of the main event. But it didn't matter, no one was listening. Watches were checked, seconds ticked by, that ferocious energy again pulsating through the crowd. Then finally, amid a roar of excitement, the cars emerged onto the track, completed their installation and warm-up laps, and took their positions on the grid.

The tension in those final seconds before the start of a race is almost unbearable. One by one the five red lights blink into life, revs build to a crescendo; the drivers utterly focused, pulses racing. For a moment, everything freezes; 22 racing cars hang in limbo, 22 pairs of eyes stare intently at the start lights, 22 clutches balanced to perfection, 100,000 spectators hold their breath, and then ... all hell breaks loose. Twenty two drivers charge down to the

first corner, battling for position in a frantic, brutal mêlée, weaving and diving like a startled school of fish. Brakes lock, tortured tyres emit plumes of smoke, the inevitable contact sending a shower of carbon fibre into the air; shattered wings scatter across the track, forcing those behind into avoiding action, creating even greater mayhem.

As the deafening shriek of the engines subsides, dust and rubber and oil hang in the air, and the crowd takes a collective breath. Say what you like about the rest of the race; the start of a Grand Prix is the single most exhilarating spectacle in the world of sport.

That evening I returned via most of Germany and much of Belgium to the little hotel in Büllingen, where I was greeted like an old friend and treated to a wonderful meal, a hot shower and, most importantly, a warm, dry bed to sleep in.

17
Go, Michael, Go!

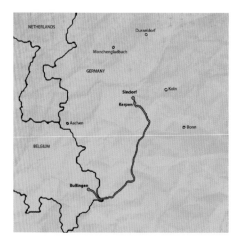

Refreshed by a good night's sleep, I came downstairs to find a lovely spread laid on for breakfast. Having again consumed my body weight in boiled eggs and toast, and drunk at least a gallon of orange juice and coffee, I somehow made it back upstairs to pack, casting a mournful eye over this haven of dryness and warmth that I was once again leaving behind.

However, before I could depart, a little surprise was waiting for me. The kindly owners, knowing of my love of motorsport, handed me a CD featuring a euro-pop tribute to Michael Schumacher. Judging by the packaging, it seemed unlikely to be an official piece of Schumacher merchandise (I

suspect the man himself remains ignorant of its existence to this day, and that's probably a good thing). Still, it felt only right that I should hear it in the company of my hosts, so I suggested it be played in the dining room while I got my luggage together. In hindsight, the proprietors' reluctance to do so was understandable, but I maintain that at the time, I had no idea how horrible the next few minutes would be.

For some things in this world there are simply no words: the mesmerising beauty of the Aurora Borealis is one of them, the Michael Company's 'Go, Michael, Go' is another. No words that adequately describe it, that is. The song itself has words; here are some of them:

'Go, Michael, go – go, Michael, go
You are the champion
You are the winner
Go, Michael, go
Go, Michael, go – go, Michael, go
You are the best one, you are the only
Therefore, Michael, go.'

That is the chorus; it happens five times. The listener is therefore left in no doubt that the sole intent of the song is to encourage Michael to go.

The first verse goes on to explain the motive behind this extraordinary tribute:

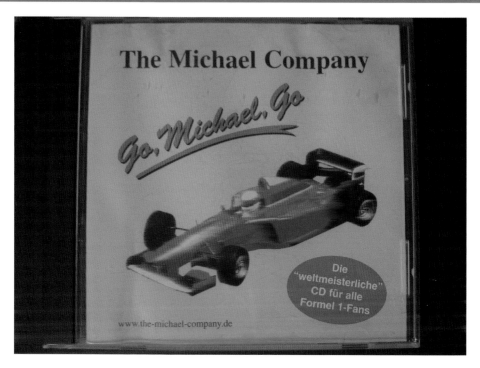

The Michael Company

Go, Michael, Go

Die "weltmeisterliche" CD für alle Formel 1-Fans

www.the-michael-company.de

Yes, it really does exist and, yes, I do still occasionally listen to it.

'Startin' from the pole-position
Michael, that's your place
Always drivin' at the limit
Michael, you're the best.'

Next comes a brief moment of confusion stemming from a careless translation, but still the message is clear:

'No one who can beat you
Cos to you belongs the race
Sunshine, rain, it doesn't matter
You are always first.'

The lyrics continue in this vein through the second verse, where the artist transcends traditional notions of rhyme in an effort to better convey his reverence to Michael:

'When you're drivin' in your car
You're never looking back
You're the best we've ever had
And you're the champ in red
See you drivin' makes us happy
You're a one-man show
That is why we love you so and
Therefore, Michael, go.'

As a gift, I have received better. In fact, as punishment I've not received worse. I didn't know what to say: 'Thank you' would have sounded sarcastic. After a grim pause I managed a genuine 'gosh,' whereupon another guest entered the room (presumably to enquire where Michael had gone?) and we were able to discreetly sweep the whole dreadful affair under the carpet.

Having bid farewell to Eddy and Marleen – and with Paul's birthday present carefully tucked into my rucksack – I consulted my maps to locate the town of Kerpen, which, as any Michael Company fan will tell you, is Schumacher's home town. I was looking forward to visiting the museum and exhibition centre built in Michael's honour and amusingly titled – in my advertising pamphlet, at least – The World of the Schumachers, which sounded like some grisly Victorian freak show. I had visions of dwarf Schumachers racing each other on the backs of wild pigs, extremely tall Schumachers with pin heads, a lady Schumacher with a beard, and perhaps even the elephant Schumacher.

Following this extravaganza, I planned to head a few kilometres south, toward the small town of Nürburg and the infamous Nordschliefe – the most daunting, formidable and challenging racetrack in the world.

Kerpen is a small town in northern Germany with one extraordinary feature; it is invisible. I state this as fact because there is no other way I could have come so close to its borders so many times and yet still managed to miss it. In my quest to find Kerpen I visited a pig farm, a petrol station, three garages, two garden centres and a supermarket, and everyone I spoke to was adamant that if I just went left here and right there I should see signposts for Kerpen in less than five minutes. Which was true: I saw signposts which intimated that Kerpen was half a mile north of me, and I saw signposts that declared the place lay half a mile south of me. I even saw a couple of signposts that welcomed me to Kerpen and hoped that I would have a pleasant stay. But even then, when, by all accounts, I stood in the heart of that town, I saw no trace of anything that was, in itself, Kerpen.

Eventually, frustrated and completely dispirited I gave up ... and immediately found myself in Kerpen, whereupon I discovered to my dismay that the Schumacher exhibition was not in Kerpen at all, but rather located in a little town called Sindorf about three miles (5km) away, to which I was led by a kindly fellow on an old Kawasaki.

It has to be said, the approach to the museum (and the attached karting track) does little to suggest that the ensuing hour or so will be anything other than dreadful, situated as it is amid a landscape peppered with dull, anonymous business parks and factories. However, appearances can be deceptive and, once inside (provided you are a Michael – or, to a lesser extent, Ralph – Schumacher fan) you will almost certainly be pleasantly surprised.

The museum is full of interesting memorabilia – overalls, crash helmets, race cars, etc – all of which are brought to life with the aid of numerous videos and a knowledgeable tour guide. At least I assume he was knowledgeable; judging by the authority of his voice and his world-weary countenance, he appeared to have conducted this tour enough times to know what he was talking about. But I cannot say for sure because I didn't understand a word he was

In the master's shadow: the karting track next to the Schumacher exhibition.

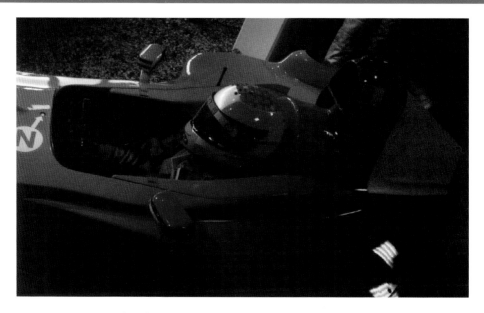

One of the many unique exhibits that I wasn't allowed to touch.

saying. Unfortunately, the English interpreter was not available on the day of my visit and the entire tour was narrated in German. At first I tried to pretend I understood what was being said, nodding and smiling along with the rest of the visitors, but eventually I gave up and wandered off to explore the exhibits on my own, whereupon I quickly discovered that the tour guide knew at least six words of English:

"YOU VILL PLEASE LEAVE ZAT ALONE!" echoed around the corridors as he spied me trying to squeeze myself into a Ferrari, slip on a crash helmet or tamper with some other piece of memorabilia.

Despite the linguistic oversight, I must say that no expense had been spared in making the place both entertaining and enjoyable, and it's well worth a visit if, like me, you're a Schumacher fan.

In the history of motorsport, I don't think there's ever been a driver who's polarised opinion like Michael Schumacher:

he's either the greatest all-round talent the sport has ever seen, or a cheat and a bully who'll tear up the rule book in his pursuit of victory. His fans will point to the statistics, arguing that you don't win seven World Championships without being consistently better than everyone else. His detractors will argue that he only won those championships because he had the best car and no competition. Which is true, to an extent. But that's overlooking a number of salient points.

Who else could have turned the dismal Ferrari team of the mid-90s into a championship-winning proposition, let alone a team that could win six Constructor's Championships in a row? If Michael had had a little more luck on his side he could have feasibly won the Driver's Championship every year from '94 to 2006 (with the exception of '96 when he moved to Ferrari and began its renaissance). It's true that, for much of his career, Schumacher did have the

Self above Schumy's pit at Monaco. I have no idea how I got up there but they wouldn't let me stay for the race.

better car, but only because he made it the best; he wasn't gifted anything. It is also true, however, that over the decade or so that he ruled Formula One, 'Schumy' had little real competition. Hakkinen was incredibly quick but, over the duration of a season, you could practically *see* him wilt. Montoya could have been a threat but he never showed anything like the commitment needed to consistently beat Schumacher. Raikkonen might have done it if the Mclaren hadn't kept breaking down, but even then, you could never imagine Kimi sticking around long once he'd lifted the big prize.

So it was left to Alonso to dethrone the king and, to be fair, he's probably the most deserving successor of them all. Alonso is just as ruthless, just as dedicated, and just as uncompromising as Schumacher. Like Michael, Alonso understands the necessity of having the whole team focused on him, not because he's afraid of having his team-mate beat him, but because he knows his talent is deserving of the team's complete attention. Alonso understands that a team doesn't win multiple World Championships by splitting its resources fairly: you focus on your best bet, the guy most likely to win most of the time. Throughout his career, no matter who his team-mate was, that person's been Alonso. Just like it was always Schumacher.

Sorry, Rubens.

18

My favourite game

My first visit to the Nürburgring, the one recorded here, was a terrifying experience, but I can honestly say that with each subsequent trip – and there have been quite a few now – the trepidation, thrill and excitement of returning to that magical place only grows.

Once you've made your way across the channel, the journey to the 'Ring is pretty straightforward, if largely dull and uneventful. Just follow the E40 towards and around Brussels, then carry on past Liége (spelt Luik on all the signposts). Exit the E40 at junction 38 and pass through Eupen, before picking up the N67 heading toward Monschau.

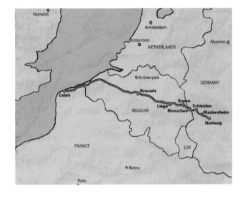

The run from Calais to Nürburg is relatively straightforward.

Signpost in Adenau showing distance to world's major racetracks.

A very welcome sign after a six hour ride from London.

After an 8km (five mile) bounce along one of the worst little roads in Europe, you'll finally escape the urban sprawl and begin a much more enjoyable ride toward the Eifel Mountains. Now you can begin to have some fun! The dull, industrial, motorway-laced landscape gives way to flowing, serpentine roads threading through lush green pine forests. Countless fast, sweeping bends beckon you in at silly speeds, bike cranked over, the trees and scrub and blackness of the forest a faintly perceived blur in your peripheral vision as your eyes strain to scan the road ahead for fallen branches and gravel. Easing off now and then as you pass through quaint German villages – Monschau, Schleiden, Blankenheim, nodding to the schoolchildren pointing from the footpaths – then back on it, tucked in behind the

screen; stupid, dangerous, impossible to resist. Finally, with a grin the size of the Karussell spread across your face, you pass either the famous petrol station or the new, tame Formula One circuit – depending on which direction you've approached from – and peel off into the tiny hamlet of Nürburg, ready for a beer and a pizza at the Pistenklause. The pilgrimage is at an end; tomorrow comes the epiphany.

If you're using a sat-nav or know your route, the run from Calais to Nürburg will take about five hours, and ideally you'll want to arrive at about four o'clock in the afternoon to allow yourself enough time to dump your luggage and prepare for one of the two-hour evening sessions that run most week days.

Unless a big event is on at the new

The little village of Nürburg is a surprisingly sleepy place to find such a tremendous track.

Nürburgring (which sits right alongside its infamous, older brother) you should be able to get a room in a local hotel. The little village of Nürburg has three or four good hotels which serve great food and strong beer. I usually stay at the Motorsport Hotel, where the staff are friendly and helpful, and you can spend a wet morning admiring the wonderful photographs that line the hallways (and the incongruous BMW motorcycle on the staircase). If you fancy something to do in the evenings, the larger town of Adenau is about six miles (10km) away. The 'Ring is usually open to the public between 5.15pm and 7.30pm weekdays, and all day at weekends, but check the official website regularly because opening times vary significantly from April to September. From experience, I'd recommend the shorter evening sessions over the manic weekends, especially if you're new to the track; you can concentrate on your own lap without worrying quite so much about what's looming in your mirrors. And while the two-hour evening sessions may not seem very long, given you've just ridden all the way from England, you'll comfortably manage three or four laps in that time, which is more than enough for a first day.

Unfortunately, when I finally pulled into the car park at the Nürburgring for the first time, I didn't know any of the above. I was drenched to the skin, having ridden through what could best be described as a monsoon for about three hours. Then I'd arrived at the wrong Nürburgring, having followed signposts to the new track. Eventually, after another 20 minutes riding round the back roads that run under and over the 'Ring, I came across the little roundabout that marks the entrance to the paddock, parked the Suzuki and removed my sodden helmet. Finally, I'd made it.

I unloaded my bags and dragged them

Parking's not a problem at the Motorsport Hotel.

over to the steps of the restaurant in the middle of the car park, whereupon I got chatting to a chap named Mick who, by a strange coincidence, happened to live about a half mile from me in south east London. He was a regular at the Nürburgring – so much so that the mere mention of his name was all I needed to get a room in a hotel that was technically closed – but his current visit had been ruined by a gang of thieves who'd stolen his bike a few days earlier. He was waiting around for a replacement to be delivered by his insurance company and, with nothing better to do, kindly offered to look after my luggage while I took to the track. I dumped my sodden belongings at

Not just for modern supercars; the owner of this pretty little Elan waits for the track to open.

Every single thing in that tailpack is drenched.

As opening time nears, the car park begins to fill and the sense of trepidation grows.

his feet and Mick gazed incredulously at the dripping mess before him. I think that in some small way it made him feel a bit better about his own loss: it was as though before meeting me, he felt things could get no worse.

That first lap, on a drenched track about which I new little, other than that it had been claiming the lives of much better riders than me for the best part of eighty years, was utterly terrifying. The Nürburgring is one of those strange places where the powers-that-be simply stand back and let people get on with killing themselves if that's what they want to do. Any fool with a blind faith in their own ability can don a crash helmet and take to the track without so much as a five minute safety briefing, and scare themselves senseless in pursuit of something that has long since been outlawed in places where life is something other people do on television.

There are no safety nets at the 'Ring; no second chances, and no pity when things go wrong, and they will. Put your balls on the line one too many times and some speed-crazed freak in a GT3 will come right up out of the mist and squash them flat to the Tarmac.

My one lap of the Nordschliefe on that wet afternoon in August was undoubtedly the slowest anyone has ever ridden round that place, but, even so, I never felt more than a moment away from disaster. Not once during that lap did I come close to pushing the bike, but similarly, there wasn't a single moment when my concentration dropped below 100 per cent. Every corner, every lean and correction felt like some strange and exotic drug. There are parts of that track that make Eau Rouge look like a speed bump; learning it, in the traditional sense, could only come with years of practice. And even then there will always be someone faster; always someone ready to push the envelope that little bit further and creep that little bit

closer to the edge of the chasm. And then, WAMMO! out come the flags.

The great Jackie Stewart, a man whose reputation has been built as much on his desire to stay alive as his undoubted driving prowess, had this to say about the Nordschleife:

"Nothing gave me more satisfaction than to win at the Nürburgring, and yet, I was always afraid. When I left home for the German Grand Prix I always used to pause at the end of the driveway and take a long look back. I was never sure I'd come home again."

"Do you want to do another lap? You can use my season ticket if you like?"

As nice a chap as Mick was, I have never met anyone so inept at reading another person's body language. I was seated at a table in the paddock restaurant, sipping coffee and feverishly trying to compose myself. A half hour had passed since I pulled off the circuit and my hands were still shaking. I caught my reflection in a window and saw staring back at me two fear-crazed eyes and a complexion so pale that even the remnants of my sunburn had disappeared.

I was in no doubt I'd pushed my luck as far as it was going to go that day. Another lap, with the adrenalin pumping and a desire to ride harder, would have been suicide. However, I did make a promise to myself there and then that I would return to the Nürburgring, and that I would attempt to ride it at something above a snail's pace. But never again would I venture onto that track in anything other than ideal conditions.

That first visit sowed the seeds of an obsession that shows no signs of waning. The 'Ring is a wonderful anachronism, a truly epic circuit situated amid vast forests that feed one's sense of history and mortality. Sadly, it seems unlikely to remain that way: *Top Gear* and *Gran Turismo* have brought the 'Ring to the masses in a manner that

The formidable Wippermann: fast, difficult, dangerous – and perfectly at home on the 'Ring.

its own marketing staff could barely have dreamt of. Since I've been returning, the infrastructure surrounding it has changed beyond all recognition. An impressive trading estate now lines the main road outside of Nürburg, populated by the likes of Ohlins, Aston Martin and Jaguar. The new track has spawned a huge entertainment facility that includes a museum, cinema, a multitude of merchandise stores, and a roller coaster that runs through the middle of the exhibition hall.

It's a far cry from the old barns that once housed the Mercedes and Auto-Unions of Rosemeyer and Caracciola and, to my mind, fundamentally at odds with the spirit and heritage of the place. The locals certainly aren't impressed: they call it 'Nürodisney'...

About the only places you won't find shiny VIP lounges, hospitality suites and over-priced shops are the ad hoc viewing areas scattered around the circuit. While these are pretty sparse, it's handy to know about them as there's often not a lot to do during the day before the track opens, and watching the professionals put brand new

The rollercoaster which runs through the complex, but which I have never actually seen in operation.

The point where the rollercoaster enters the exhibition centre.

The rather soulless – and very contentious – new complex, nicknamed Nürodisney by the locals owing to its family-themed attractions.

supercars through their paces is a good way to pass the time. The most accessible viewing spot is probably at the bridge on the way to Adenau, but it's also worth popping down to the dusty car park that overlooks the fast downhill right-hander at Brunchen; Pflanzgarten isn't far from here, either.

To get to the viewing spot at Adenau bridge, come out of the Nürburgring car park and take the first exit at the roundabout, then follow the road for about 0.6 of a mile (1km) until it ends in a T-junction. Turn left and then follow a great little road for about three miles (5km). Watch out for the three

Pflanzgarten – a wonderful section of track.

Ex-Mühle – a tricky little bend that I've yet to get right.

very tight hairpins, the last of which is about 100 yards (90 metres) from the end of the road. This time, at the T-junction turn right and follow this larger road for about a mile and a half (2.5km) until you come to a car park and café – which sells some unusual 'Ring stickers – on your right and another restaurant on your left. Park up and you'll see a big mural of some motorbikes next to a bridge and steps alongside it. The bridge is actually carrying the Nürburgring over the road, so head up those steps for a great view of the track. Alternatively, head around the back of the café and you'll be within spitting distance of Ex-Mühle, a tricky, uphill right-hander that I always take in the wrong gear.

If you get bored of watching from Adenau, head back toward Nürburg and –

again from the 'Ring car park – turn right and follow the road for about a kilometre until you reach the above-mentioned T-junction. This time, turn right and almost immediately you'll come to another T-junction where you'll turn left (go right for the famous petrol station that sells all manner of 'Ring memorabilia, including pasta!). Having turned left onto the main road, follow it for about three quarters of a mile (1.2km) before taking the first exit on the left (signposted Hohe Acht – if you're staying at the Berghotel you'll be going this way anyway). After about half a mile (0.8km), pull on to the unpaved car park on your right and you'll find yourself opposite the Pflanzgarten section of the 'Ring. This is a great viewing spot, as the jump just

Brünnchen: don't forget to wave.

before the sweeping right-hander can really unsettle a car or bike. From here you can walk all the way around to the infamous Karussell, but be warned, it's quite a way and the ground is pretty rough. Head back onto the same road for another half mile or so and you'll see on your left the dusty car park which constitutes the viewing area for Brunchen.

Accidents happen, and when they do, they tend to be expensive.

So you've decided your car or bike needs a squiggly little sticker on it and you're planning a trip to the 'Ring. The first thing you should do is visit Ben Lovejoy's website (http://www.nurburgring.org.uk/): it's totally comprehensive and the best 'how to do the 'Ring' guide you'll find anywhere. While my knowledge of the 'Ring pales in comparison, I'd suggest the following tips to any first-time visitor.

Read the rules of the track, which you'll find near the ticket office in the 'Ring car park. They'll tell you what the flags mean, that you need to indicate and pull to the right to let faster vehicles overtake, and basically not to be an idiot.

Opening times can be found on the official website: http://www.nuerburgring.de/en/angebote/driving-experiences/tourist-rides-nordschleife/opening-times-nordschleife.html

Download the free safety booklet from Ben's website (http://www.nurburgring.org.uk/safety-leaflet.pdf), and don't forget to put the emergency number into your phone.

Six minute laps on the PlayStation don't count for much in the real word. Take it steady, keep an eye on your mirrors, and don't get carried away. However, if you fancy a little virtual practice, the Nordschleife download (http://www.nogripracing.com/details.php?filenr=1913) for GT Legends and GTR 2 on the PC is as close as a video game can get in my opinion. It's also worth watching a few onboard laps on YouTube, if for no other reason than to get an idea of just how long the track is.

Make sure your vehicle's safe, not only for you but for everyone else, too. In particular, check that it isn't dripping fluids: ignoring a slight oil leak could put the guy behind you in hospital, or worse.

Enjoy yourself. The best way to do so, at least on your first visit, is by riding or driving safely, enjoying the local food and drink and soaking up the beautiful scenery when the track's closed. Part of the 'Ring's appeal lies in its location; utterly removed from the banality of everyday life. You don't need to be doing 150mph to appreciate that. Of course, the worst way to see the 'Ring is from the back of an ambulance, and while the staff at the Krankenhaus in Adenau are very friendly, there's only so many broken Brits they can patch up before their sympathy starts to wane.

Oh, and don't accidently go to Nuremberg, which is hundreds of kilometres away in a different part of Germany (although you wouldn't be the first).

Me on a later trip, tipping it in to the Karussell. You'll find a number of photographers' sites at: http://www.nordschleifepics.com/.

19

Homeward bound

30th August

Strange feelings ran through my mind on that bright, sunny morning in the heart of the Eifel Mountains. I'd woken early, excited and saddened in equal measure as my trip was almost at an end; tomorrow I'd be back in London, amid the taxis and the smog. But at that moment, sat astride my bike, overlooking the shimmering, silver straight of the Nurburgring, I was still a million miles away.

I'd spent the last hour or so exploring the decrepit castle which sits mournfully on the hilltop overlooking Nurburg, built back in the 12th century by Count Ulrich von Nurburg. From its turret, the views are stunning: almost directly below is the new Grand Prix complex, shiny and modern and seemingly at odds with the surrounding countryside. But lift your eyes to the horizon, look beyond the steel and asphalt, and you can practically step back in time, before factories and motorways and urban sprawl, to the days when the Count gazed out across his kingdom of forests and fields; to a time when the 'Ring was just grass-covered contour waiting to be revealed.

I was alone up there on top of the tower, with no one to tell me when or where or how to be. Just me and the clouds and the breeze. It's how I feel when I pull on my crash helmet and close the visor. Alone and at peace.

I looked out beyond Nurburg, past Adenau, beyond the rolling hills and the Eifel Mountains, beyond Germany even, to Europe – a vast, sweeping mass of triumph and tragedy, romance and despair, heroism and tyranny; as diverse geographically as it is culturally. This way for scorching Mediterranean beaches, that way for the snow-capped Alps and great swathes of green forest. An eclectic playground of excitement and challenge – and I had barely scratched the surface. Still, the time had come to say goodbye, for now, at least. With a heavy heart I made my way back down the castle's spiral staircase, through its ruined walls and along the pathway to where I'd left the Suzuki leaning heavily on its side-stand. After a final look around, I slid the key into

Like so much around Nürburg, the old castle is steeped in history and tradition.

the ignition, dabbed the starter, and with the sweltering heat of the Mediterranean now a distant memory, reluctantly began the final leg of my journey back to London.

31 August

It was a shame that I spent the final night of my trip in Calais. In hindsight, I should have stayed somewhere more remote, or at least less obvious. It's no wonder the French have a slightly jaundiced view of the English, when we stampede over to poor old Calais in search of cheap booze and fags, *Daily Mails* stuffed into XXL tracksuits, and drinking Stella on the ferry at half nine in the morning just because we can.

Like most coastal towns, Calais has a fascinating history, and was part of England

Spectacular views from the top of the castle, although surprisingly, very little of the 'Ring is visible.

Sunrise over Nürburg: what must Fangio or Caracciola have felt as they prepared for race day?

from the mid-fourteenth century until the French reclaimed it in 1558. It was probably beautiful until the Nazis flattened it in the early stages of World War II, although its sacrifice undoubtedly helped those fleeing Dunkirk, as the Panzer division that razed it would otherwise have been shelling the retreating allies.

Now it exists as a sad and depressing wasteland; somewhere to get through on the way to someplace better, its chequered past well and truly buried under cheap pizzerias and tatty arcades.

As it was, I spent my last night 'on the road' in a tired hotel a stone's throw from Dover, wishing for all the world I was back in Nürburg or Monaco or Lerici, or Bolzano even. I strolled down to the docks to watch the sun set, then grabbed a bottle of wine and retreated to my hotel, where I lay awake for half the night worrying that my bike was being stolen.

The next morning, I made my way to the ferry port and waited for my ship to come in. To kill time I began to re-read my notes, and it struck me, in a paradoxical sort

Watching sadly as the sun sets for the last time on my journey.

Early morning in Calais: a fine day for a motorcycle ride.

of way, how long and yet how short a month can be. On the one hand, that early morning ride to Dover seemed unimaginably distant, whilst, on the other, the month seemed to have passed in little more than the blink of an eye. So much had happened, although, in many ways, so little. In reality, I'd spent four weeks taking in tourist sites and getting lost, but, clichéd as it may be, it was those times of tribulation that now stood out as the highlights of the trip. Lost in France, lost in Italy, lost in Austria and Belgium, too, but somehow still alive and grateful with it. Okay, I hadn't exactly slummed it, and I'm sure travelling across Thailand or India has its fair share of challenges, too, but I'd done what I'd set out to do and in my own small way I felt slightly, embarrassingly, proud of myself.

Next to me, resting on its side-stand, stood my Suzuki, which had really done the hard work. Its fairing and screen were splattered with a rain forest's worth of bugs, while its poor suspension sagged under the weight of my luggage. I swung my leg over the seat and sank into that familiar position, just as I had done 4000 miles ago at the start of the journey. We waited together like old friends, until finally, after what seemed like an age, the ferry docked and for the first time in a month, the wheels of my bike left continental Europe.

Ready for the final leg.

At 1.30pm on a sunny afternoon in August, a dirty, battered Suzuki SV650S with an equally mucky rider, rode down the exit ramp of the Pride of Dover on to English soil and pulled up next to the customs desk. The fellow behind the glass looked at my passport and frowned:

"Remove your crash helmet, please sir." he instructed. I did as I was asked, half hoping that some bureaucratic mix-up would force me onto the next ferry back to France.

"This *is* you, is it, sir?"

I looked at him, confused and a little taken aback.

"Certainly is," I replied.

"Doesn't really look like you, sir," he answered, turning the passport to face me.

To be fair, the last month had taken its toll. I hadn't shaved for quite a while, and I'm pretty sure I'd washed my hair at some point in the three weeks prior to the photo being taken. Still, it was clearly me and I wasn't really in the mood for ponderous bureaucracy. I adopted an expression which said:

"Do your duty if you must, but be warned, I am not to be trifled with. I have just spent the last month living in a tent 12 inches too small for me and which positively beckoned the rain inside like a lost friend. I have survived tidal waves and sunstroke, Italian road signs, French swimming pools, Belgian race fans and a host of other petty annoyances that would have driven a lesser man to murder. I am in no mood to pander to your pompous delusions. Let me on my way and we'll say no more about the matter."

I should say I had mastered that look, because he handed back my passport and raised the barrier without another word. I thanked him and replaced my crash helmet, and then I clunked the Suzuki into first gear and rode away, back down the M20, towards London and home.

I bought a couple of croissants and a cup of something resembling coffee and made my way up on deck to watch, sadly, as the continent slowly receded. Actually 'slowly' doesn't quite do the pace of that ferry justice: it seemed to be inching, rather than powering, out to sea. After the best part of 20 minutes, not only could I still see the port, I could probably have jumped back onto it with a good run-up. Eventually, though, those famous white cliffs appeared on the horizon, and a while later, with a pang of regret, I found myself back in England.

Body, home; mind, far away in a place where the only sounds are the rushing wind and the growl of a V-twin.

Where it all Began – the Honda CG125
Like many people, my first bike was a Honda CG125. My mate, Rich, sold it to me after he graduated to a larger machine (a Virago 535cc – I had one, too, and they're good fun, if a little prone to understeer). The CG125 is one of the all-time great motorbikes in my opinion. Perfect to learn on, you can crash it to your heart's content and nothing serious will ever go wrong (a mechanic once told me how he'd drained the engine oil out of a CG125 and then started it to see how long it would last; it ran out of petrol before anything more catastrophic happened). It's also easy to work on, great fun to ride, and incredibly economical: for the first few weeks of owning mine I thought I'd been sold a perpetual motion machine. In almost every practical way the little Honda was better than any other bike I've ever owned; unfortunately, that practically carries over to the styling, or rather lack of — no one has ever impressed a girl riding a CG125.

A great little bike.

Epilogue

I have often wondered what is the point of an epilogue? The story has ended, the book is complete; there is nothing left to say. But then one stumbles across this little fellow, tagged on to the end like some unwanted orphan, a kind of apologetic secondary finale.

As I write this, some months after my return, seated at my desk in East Dulwich and staring out upon a cold winter's morning, the beaches of southern France and the sweltering heat of Rome seem a world away. But I know now they are not. They are in this world, and really not that far away at all.

I think about that journey, for all its mishaps and tribulations, with a degree of fondness one would reserve for an old friend. Like a trusted companion, that trip failed in any way to make me a better person, and rarely demanded from me anything more than that I sit down and enjoy a nice bottle of red wine. In fact, I feel sure that were I to have 'discovered myself' or experienced anything remotely transcendental, the whole trip would have been ruined and I would have come home a failure. As it is, I am none the wiser about myself and all the better for it.

Although, perhaps that is not entirely true. At the very least, my motorcycle journey taught me that a few common hand gestures can overcome the most troublesome linguistic barriers, that I was right in my belief that camping has no redeeming features, and that there are enough good and decent people scattered across this world to ensure a helping hand is never far away.

Come to think of it, perhaps that is the point of an epilogue.

The end

PS, I saw Nina once more after my visit to her family's house in Stuttgart. Back in London she invited me to a party where, after a few drinks, I managed to spill a bottle of red wine over the cream carpet. I left without a kiss goodnight; seems it wasn't meant to be.

Big thank you to everyone who helped me along the way!

Acknowledgements

Thanks to:
Dad, for teaching me that an oil filter's nothing to be afraid of, and for so much more; Amy, for saying yes; Mike for the anecdotes and proofing services; Sam and Amy for the illustrations/maps; Dave, for the waterproofs, etc; Rich for the tank bag and Bob because I've mentioned Rich; Mr & Mrs Carrier for their hospitality; all the nice people who told me where to go; Simon the mechanic and his mate; Mick the courier and Renate, proprietor of the Gasthaus Lindenh in Nurburg; Jon Blackburn and Kevin and Jude at Veloce, for their inexhaustible patience; Suzuki for the SV650S; the chap who invented the internet, without whom this book would be entirely devoid of facts; Barry, Hannah and Laura for looking after the plants and not moving house while I was away.

Chin-chin!

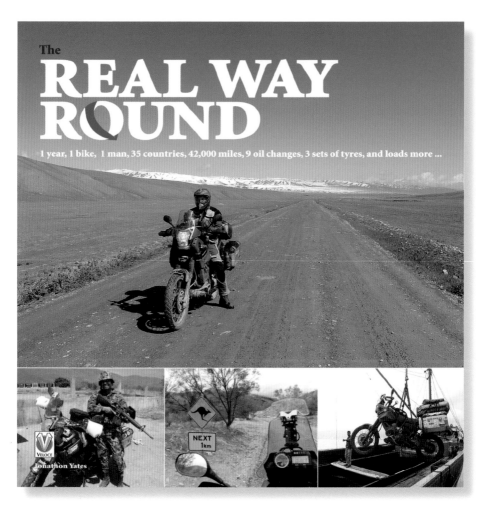

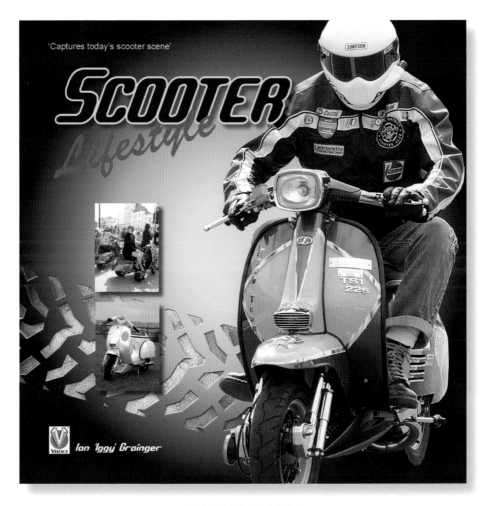

ISBN: 978-1-84584-152-2
Paperback · 25x25cm · £19.99* UK/$39.95* USA · 128 pages · 380 colour and b&w pictures

For more info on Veloce titles, visit our website at www.veloce.co.uk · email: info@veloce.co.uk ·
Tel: +44(0)1305 260068
* prices subject to change, p&p extra

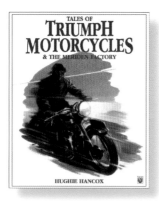

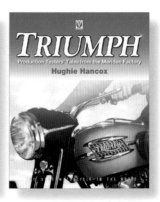

ISBN: 978-1-901295-67-2
Paperback · 25x20.7cm ·
£19.99* UK/$39.95* USA · 144
pages · pictures

ISBN: 978-1-84584-179-9
Hardback · 25x20.7cm · £19.99*
UK/$39.95* USA · 128 pages ·
102 colour and b&w pictures

ISBN: 978-1-845844-41-7
Paperback · 25x20.7cm ·
£19.99* UK/$39.95* USA ·
160 pages · 183 colour and b&w
pictures

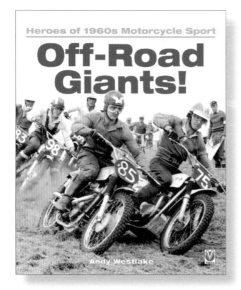

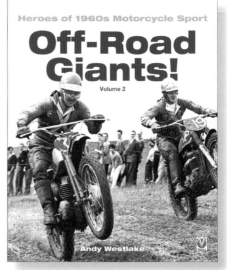

ISBN: 978-1-84584-190-4
Hardback · 25x20.7cm · £19.99* UK/$39.95*
USA · 128 pages · 115 b&w pictures

ISBN: 978-1-845843-23-6
Hardback · 25x20.7cm · £19.99* UK/$39.95*
USA · 128 pages · 123 b&w pictures

For more info on Veloce titles, visit our website at www.veloce.co.uk · email: info@veloce.co.uk ·
Tel: +44(0)1305 260068
* prices subject to change, p&p extra

ISBN: 978-1-845843-25-0
Hardback · 25x25cm · £19.99*
UK/$39.95* USA · 128 pages · 270
colour and b&w pictures

ISBN: 978-1-845843-94-6
Hardback · 25x25cm · £19.99*
UK/$39.95* USA · 128 pages · 260
colour and b&w pictures

For more info on Veloce titles, visit our website at www.veloce.co.uk · email: info@veloce.co.uk ·
Tel: +44(0)1305 260068
* prices subject to change, p&p extra

Index

Other great motorcycle related books from Veloce –

Harley-Davidson Evolution Engines, How to Build & Power Tune (Hammill)
Motorcycle-engined Racing Car, How to Build (Pashley)
Classic Large Frame Vespa Scooters, How to Restore (Paxton)
Ducati Bevel Twins 1971 to 1986 (Falloon)
Yamaha FS1-E, How to Restore (Watts)
BSA Bantam (Henshaw)
BSA 500 & 650 Twins (Henshaw)
Ducati Bevel Twins (Falloon)
Harley-Davidson Big Twins (Henshaw)
Hinckley Triumph triples & fours 750, 900, 955, 1000, 1050, 1200 – 1991-2009 (Henshaw)
Honda CBR600 Hurricane (Henshaw)
Honda CBR FireBlade (Henshaw)
Honda SOHC fours 1969-1984 (Henshaw)
Triumph Bonneville (Henshaw)
Vespa Scooters – Classic 2-stroke models 1960-2008 (Paxton)
Café Racer Phenomenon, The (Walker)
Drag Bike Racing in Britain – From the mid '60s to the mid '80s (Lee)
Edward Turner – The Man Behind the Motorcycles (Clew)
Jim Redman – 6 Times World Motorcycle Champion: The Autobiography (Redman)
BMW Custom Motorcycles (Cloesen)
British 250cc Racing Motorcycles (Pereira)
BSA Bantam Bible, The (Henshaw)
Ducati 750 Bible, The (Falloon)
Ducati 750 SS 'round-case' 1974, The Book of the (Falloon)

Ducati 860, 900 and Mille Bible, The (Falloon)
Ducati Monster Bible, The (Falloon)
Fine Art of the Motorcycle Engine, The (Peirce)
Funky Mopeds (Skelton)
Italian Custom Motorcycles (Cloesen)
Kawasaki Triples Bible, The (Walker)
little book of trikes, the (Quellin)
Moto Guzzi Sport & Le Mans Bible, The (Falloon)
Motorcycle Apprentice (Cakebread)
Motorcycle GP Racing in the 1960s (Pereira)
Motorcycle Road & Racing Chassis Designs (Noakes)
MV Agusta Fours, The book of the classic (Falloon)
Off-Road Giants! (Volume 1) – Heroes of 1960s Motorcycle Sport (Westlake)
Off-Road Giants! (Volume 2) – Heroes of 1960s Motorcycle Sport (Westlake)
Scooters & Microcars, The A-Z of Popular (Dan)
Scooter Lifestyle (Grainger)
Singer Story: Cars, Commercial Vehicles, Bicycles & Motorcycle (Atkinson)
Triumph Bonneville Bible (59-83) (Henshaw)
Triumph Bonneville!, Save the – The inside story of the Meriden Workers' Co-op (Rosamond)
Triumph Motorcycles & the Meriden Factory (Hancox)
Triumph Speed Twin & Thunderbird Bible (Woolridge)
Triumph Tiger Cub Bible (Estall)
Triumph Trophy Bible (Woolridge)

www.veloce.co.uk

First published in May 2012 by Veloce Publishing Limited, Veloce House, Parkway Farm Business Park, Middle Farm Way, Poundbury, Dorchester, Dorset, DT1 3AR, England.
Fax 01305 250479/e-mail info@veloce.co.uk/web www.veloce.co.uk or www.velocebooks.com.

ISBN: 978-1-845843-99-1 UPC: 6-36847-04399-5

BONJOUR_!
IS THIS ITALY?

A HAPLESS BIKER'S GUIDE TO EUROPE

Kevin Turner